Journalism

by Arionne Nettles

Journalism For Dummies®

Published by: **John Wiley & Sons, Inc.,** 111 River Street, Hoboken, NJ 07030-5774, www.wiley.com

Published simultaneously in Canada

For general information on our other products and services, please contact our Customer Care Department within the U.S. at 877-762-2974, outside the U.S. at 317-572-3993, or fax 317-572-4002. For technical support, please visit https://hub.wiley.com/community/support/dummies.

Wiley publishes in a variety of print and electronic formats and by print-on-demand. Some material included with standard print versions of this book may not be included in e-books or in print-on-demand. If this book refers to media that is not included in the version you purchased, you may download this material at http://booksupport.wiley.com. For more information about Wiley products, visit www.wiley.com.

Library of Congress Control Number: 2024951735

ISBN 978-1-394-27959-3 (pbk); ISBN 978-1-394-27961-6 (ebk);
ISBN 978-1-394-27960-9 (ebk)

SKY10093711_121224

Table of Contents

PART 4: USING DIFFERENT MEDIA PLATFORMS 179

Introduction

Journalism is more than just a form of storytelling. It's how we hold powerful people accountable, how we engage the public, and how we share information with the masses. Like the famed Ida B. Wells once said, "The people must know before they can act, and there is no educator to compare with the press."

This idea has been true since the industry's inception. But even as this premise remains, *how* to do journalism is something that is ever-changing. Journalism is an extremely wide-ranging industry, with evolution happening quickly in every single part of it.

That's why this book exists. Whether you're a college student studying journalism, a recent grad looking for or starting your first journalism job, or a freelance writer wanting to hone your journalism skills, this book is for you.

About This Book

This book is a guide that explores journalistic standards and practices, as well as how journalists are currently expanding these measures. This is not a journalism book of the past, telling you how to think, how to act, and how to work. Instead, it explores how we've tackled big journalistic issues in the past and how people handle them today, while also discussing the promise of journalism as being the bedrock of democracy.

That may seem like an exaggeration, but I don't believe it is. The core of journalism is truth, accuracy, and fairness. And when I became a journalist, it was because I wanted to be committed to these foundational practices while working to grow them.

I wrote this book to equip you with the same knowledge. It's the book I wish I'd had when I was navigating the industry early on.

Within this book, you may note that some web addresses break across two lines of text. If you're reading this book in print and want to visit one of these web pages, simply key in the web address exactly as it's noted in the text, pretending as though the line break doesn't exist. If you're reading this as an e-book, you've got it easy — just click the web address to be taken directly to the web page.

Foolish Assumptions

When writing this book, I made some assumptions about you:

- **You may be a college student studying journalism or considering a career in journalism.** There is a lot to remember when it comes to this field. You just need a guide to help you reference what you're learning.
- **You may be a recent graduate, either looking for or working in your first journalism job.** The world of journalism is expansive and still growing. You can use this book to stay on top of trends as you build your career.
- **You may be a freelance writer interested in honing your journalism skills.** I initially started as a freelance writer before going back to school for journalism and, for years, there was a lot I didn't know. This book can help you keep up with what's going on in newsrooms and help you seek out opportunities.

Icons Used in This Book

This book includes icons in the margins that help to highlight information that is especially important — information I don't want you to miss.

Anything marked by the Tip icon helps you do these something better. Many of these tips are ones that I personally use and have been given by my own teachers, mentors, and editors.

There's a lot to remember when it comes to how journalists do this work. The Remember icon indicates something you'll want to commit to memory.

The Warning icons identifies anything that could be potentially problematic or make your work more difficult.

When I delve into technical topics, I mark them with the Technical Stuff icon. If you're short on time, you can safely skip anything marked with this icon without missing the essentials.

Beyond the Book

In addition to the information in this book, you get access to even more help and information online at `Dummies.com`. Check out this book's Cheat Sheet for a checklist of items to keep in your reporting bag, info on what to expect at a press conference, tips on how to decipher (and write) a press release, and tips for how to use your smartphone while reporting. Just go to `www.dummies.com` and type **Journalism For Dummies Cheat Sheet** in the Search box.

You can also find a story-planning template that you can download and use to assemble the information you need to write any story. Go to `www.dummies.com/go/journalismfd` to download it.

Where to Go from Here

This book has a ton of information, but it isn't linear. You can start anywhere. If you want an understanding of how the public takes in the information journalists produce, head to Chapter 3. For a great primer on story formats, turn to Chapter 4. To look at how ethics comes into play in journalists' work, check out Chapter 10. For suggestions on using your journalism skills in other related fields, head to Chapter 18.

For even more journalism information, recent lectures and presentations, and other helpful resources, you can also visit me online at `http://professorarionne.com`.

Onward!

1 Getting Started with Journalism

IN THIS PART . . .

Find out what is and isn't journalism while thinking through the ethical responsibility of the role of reporter.

Take a look at media literacy, what it is, and why it's an important part of journalism and democracy.

IN THIS CHAPTER

- » Getting into the field
- » Understanding your responsibility as a journalist
- » Knowing what you need to be successful

Chapter 1 Becoming a Journalist

Journalism is better when it's filled with people of all backgrounds, living in all locations, and thinking in all kinds of ways. That's why it's so exciting that *yours* will be one of the industry's next voices.

But it's important to recognize that part of becoming a journalist does involve understanding all of the career pathways and tools to help you get your foot in the door.

In this chapter, I discuss how to start a career in journalism — including the common roadblocks many people encounter and the newer ways people are tackling them.

Exploring the Many Roads to Journalism

As a field, journalism was once seen as a trade anyone could enter. Not only could aspiring writers and broadcasters study at the university level, but they also had more opportunities to learn as apprentices on the job and in training programs created by media organizations.

In recent decades, this barrier to entry has become way higher, with many competitive roles at mainstream newsrooms going to graduates of elite journalism university programs and media entities no longer willing to train new journalists.

But now, today, we are seeing an emergence of opportunities for new journalists to join the industry — in nonprofit newsrooms, through independent work on social media, and from becoming media entrepreneurs themselves. For example, it's extremely common today to see journalists solely post coverage of events and subject matter on social media instead of on a news website. The prevalence of online and digital tools means that, with the right training, the door is open for you.

The traditional road

Generally, getting a journalism job in a mainstream U.S. media organization (a TV news station, newspaper, major magazine, or radio station) means proving to its hiring managers that you already know enough about the field to be a good addition to its newsroom. For most new journalists, that can be tough. How do you prove you can do a job you haven't yet been given the chance to do?

In the following sections, I cover ways new journalists often get noticed for these positions.

Attending journalism school

School is still one of the most traditional ways of learning journalism, building a portfolio, and making connections with those in the industry. It's not the only way, but attaining an undergraduate or graduate degree is still popular. However, the cost of this route is high and it isn't always financially viable.

Participating in campus media

Many journalists get their first real experience working on stories for their campus newspapers, magazines, radio stations, and TV stations. Here, they have the benefit of covering events and happenings at a place extremely familiar to them, guided by student editors who remember what it's like to be brand-new at reporting stories. Journalists working at these media organizations must be students, but they don't necessarily have to be part of the institution's journalism program because the organization's student editors generally train reporters themselves.

Doing internships and fellowships

These types of roles are often journalists' first professional newsroom experiences. Internships are often three to six months in length and are for current students and those who have graduated within the past year. Fellowships are generally for journalists with little to no experience and can be about a year long. There are also special fellowships that seek to help journalists from underrepresented groups, as well as fellowships that train journalists in a certain area in order to increase the number of journalists working in that area. Examples include fellowships for students from historically Black colleges and other minority-serving institutions and fellowships for science reporting.

TIP

Many fellowships are for recent graduates, but that's not always the case. Some fellowships are created for other people in need of experience, such as career-changers. So, even if you're not sure you're an ideal fit, apply anyway!

Joining journalism organizations

If you ask many people in journalism what has been their best medium for meeting and staying in touch with other journalists over the years, they'll likely mention one of several professional affinity organizations. Many will also mention how an organization helped them land their first role and how they're committed to helping new journalists do the same. The networking that these groups can provide is second to none, and it's common for people to attend at least one annual conference per year.

Some journalism organizations were specifically created to support underrepresented groups, including the following:

- **Asian American Journalists Association (AAJA):** www.aaja.org
- **Association of LGBTQ+ Journalists (NLGJA):** www.nlgja.org
- **National Association of Black Journalists (NABJ):** https://nabjonline.org
- **National Association of Hispanic Journalists (NAHJ):** https://nahj.org

Other organizations are focused on certain areas of journalism:

- **Association of Health Care Journalists (AHCJ):** https://healthjournalism.org
- **Investigative Reporters & Editors (IRE):** www.ire.org
- **Online News Association (ONA):** https://journalists.org
- **Public Media Journalists Association (PMJA):** www.pmja.org

Be sure to check with each organization to see if there are local chapters near you. The national organizations provide the opportunity to connect with people across the United States and often beyond, but local chapters can give you a much more personal welcome, with resources tailored to journalists in your area.

Forging new paths

The traditional routes into journalism may still remain, but that doesn't mean there aren't new ways to get in. With every new digital trend, another journalism opening emerges.

In the following sections, I offer suggestions on how to work toward getting noticed, even if you're creating your own path.

Attending a training or certificate program

There may not be as many training programs for journalists outside the traditional degree programs at universities, but there are different programs to train people for specific kinds of work. For example, broadcast institutes can teach people how to engineer and produce radio or TV shows. There are also writing certificate programs — and with the expansion and wide acceptance of online learning, this area is quickly growing.

Be sure to vet any journalism training program, especially any that requires payment or tuition. Ask for information about people who have completed the program before and see what information you can find about the organization offering the program in the news. Are its founders seen as industry leaders? Is it a new and innovative approach to teaching or something that's tried-and-true? Make sure the investment is worth it.

Doing freelance work

The best practice you can get as a new journalist is real-world work as a freelancer. Freelance work especially helps when you don't get the opportunity to have internships or work for a student newspaper. Freelance work builds your portfolio, and you can continue to replace your work with better work as you get bigger and better opportunities — opportunities that align closer with what you want to do. It's most likely that this work will be digital or online compared to print, TV, or radio.

When I was first transitioning into journalism from working in another field, I quickly realized I needed a portfolio of work. I started taking very low-paying work just to get experience (because I had none at all) and then started to raise the caliber of assignments I would take as I got better and better, swapping out the older work in my portfolio for new and better work to share.

Connecting with other journalists

Staying connected with other journalists is the best way to find freelance work, stay up-to-date with the industry, and get career advice. Facebook, Slack, Google Groups — anywhere people gather online you're likely to find journalism groups. Many of these groups exist specifically to help journalists with certain focuses, like those who are freelance magazine writers, or journalists with certain life experiences, like those who are parents.

Because people spend hours running them, some of these groups may have small subscription fees, but most are generally free. Even the paid groups often have scholarships or sliding-scale options to help them be even more affordable because the goal is often to help journalists get work.

TIP

I've found that spending a couple of dollars a month for a subscription is usually a financial benefit for me as a freelancer in the long run. It's extremely difficult to scour the internet and social media sites and then pull together opportunities to share with other journalists, so I greatly appreciate the work that goes into it. But also, even if I tried, I usually wouldn't be able to find all the opportunities that are best for me. If I get at least one good assignment from one of those groups, then the investment more than paid for itself.

Understanding the Responsibility of a Journalist

Being a journalist is a huge deal — not just for those of us who get to do the work we want to do, but for the communities and individuals whose stories we have the honor of telling.

This line of work is an enormous responsibility. When a journalist publishes a story, it becomes part of recorded history. Think about how you would research an event that happened decades ago. You'd likely look through news coverage and try to see if you could get as many details as possible. In that case, you're trusting that the information you're seeing is factual. That's because the journalists who were there are your eyes and ears. What they reported gets you as close as possible to being there. So, you're hoping — and trusting — they did everything they could to get it right.

Similarly, *we* are the chroniclers of our time. That's why we try so hard to be truthful, accurate, and fair in our reporting. People are trusting us and relying on our work.

Regardless of what kind of journalism we practice or what medium we work in, we all have the same charge.

Being truthful

Being truthful in journalism means more than just not lying. It means ensuring that we aren't intentionally — or unintentionally — misleading our audience.

Here are some basic ways to start thinking about how truth can show itself in your work.

- **Ensure the headlines you're using are not misleading or missing content.** With so much happening in our world, many people only read the headlines of stories. They take in the headline and assume that it's a true summary of what the rest of the story is about. That's why clickbait headlines — those that are written cleverly just to get people to click on them — are untruthful. When you write a headline that is misleading, you are *not* being truthful.
- **Lay out information in a way that doesn't change the story's meaning.** Structuring stories is both a skill and an art. There are some rules around what works for different types of stories, but it really does take practice to ensure that we aren't accidentally misconstruing the truth in the order and word choice we use.
- **Choose images that best reflect the story's content.** Photos video stills, and other illustrations tell a lot about what a story will be about. Although you can be unintentionally misleading in a variety of ways, making an error is most likely when you're using stock images. For example, in

a story that examines a new health-care procedure, think about the issues of truthfulness with the following photos:

- A photo of people smiling tells audiences that the procedure is a good one. But what if the procedure is new and hasn't yet been proven?
- A photo of people looking upset says to audiences that the procedure is bad or dangerous. This photo could cause people to fear the procedure before examining the facts.
- A close-up photo of someone preparing to get a vaccine shows no faces and doesn't make a strong editorial statement.

Being accurate

Accuracy is one of the most important tenets of journalism for a reason. People are counting on journalists to get it right. We're often cited in other people's work, too, so a mistake in a news article could lead to a mistake in a book, a research paper, or another kind of scholarship that people consume.

And today, in a digital world where breaking news is expected to be shared as soon as possible, the opportunity for mistakes in accuracy has been widened. The checks and balances that used to be in place to catch such errors are no longer present in many newsrooms, and it can feel as if everyone is in a race to get information out the fastest.

TIP

But, when it comes to accuracy, you can prevent many mistakes by slowing down and taking some extra steps:

» **Double-check the spelling of names, places, and proper nouns.** Checking your spelling isn't just something to do as you're starting your story. It should also be a major step to complete at the end of your process, and it should be separate from any other checks such as reading for typos, for example. Going through and looking up each proper noun should be a final step all by itself to ensure no name is missed.

We often talk about checking the accuracy of names in written work such as print and digital stories, but remember that it's equally as important in video and audio. You can't go back and redo some mistakes that are made in these mediums, especially, and corrections are difficult to make in a way that audiences notice them. It's also extremely embarrassing when you make these errors because the people mentioned in your story can feel as if you didn't put time and effort into a story that's about them.

- **Do your math twice.** Even if you consider yourself a whiz at numbers, always do any math in your story at least twice. This includes calculations such as percentages, percentage point changes, and averages. Using a spreadsheet helps keep these calculations in a single place and makes it easier to go back and check that the formulas and numbers are correct.
- **Make sure that social media posts are just as accurate as the stories themselves.** Some people are highly accurate in a story and then fail to give that same care to social media posts. Similar to headlines, people often share social media posts without clicking through to the full story, so it's really important that any information used in a social media post is correct.

When I worked at a wire service, accuracy was a top priority because not only were our stories being read by audiences, but they were being sent to other media organizations to use. When it came to social media, we had the same standards we had for any story. And before posting on social media, it was our process to have at least one other person read what you were planning to post. We did this for every single post on every single social media platform. Don't be afraid to ask for help or get a second opinion, too.

Being fair

Fairness is not always as cut-and-dried as truthfulness and accuracy because it can mean different things to different people. But what matters is checking your own moral compass and ensuring that you're being fair to multiple sides of an issue by considering their perspectives. Be sure to do the following:

- **Check your biases.** Although some people believe in the old-school belief that journalists can be completely objective, many of us understand that we all have our own experiences and opinions, which can create biases. It's impossible to separate who we are from the work we can do. But what we can do is recognize those biases, and then, being aware of them, think through ways to ensure we aren't letting them cloud our judgment and impede our work.
- **Consider multiple sides of each issue in proportion.** When you're doing a story, especially a very newsy story, it's important to not report only on a single side. Thinking about more than one side doesn't mean that you have to give it equal weight in your final story. In the past, the journalistic standard used to be to always report "both sides" of an issue. But this "both-sidesism" can be harmful by creating a false equivalence in controversial issues, so journalists have been pushing back on this thinking and, instead, striving to put things into perspective and in proportion.

WARNING

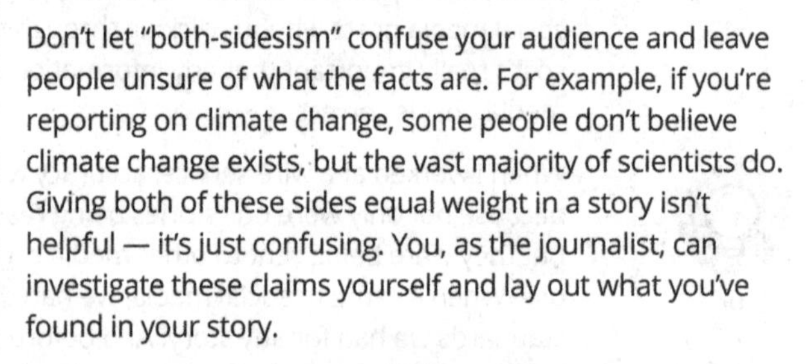

Don't let "both-sidesism" confuse your audience and leave people unsure of what the facts are. For example, if you're reporting on climate change, some people don't believe climate change exists, but the vast majority of scientists do. Giving both of these sides equal weight in a story isn't helpful — it's just confusing. You, as the journalist, can investigate these claims yourself and lay out what you've found in your story.

- **Talk to more people than you think you need to.** It's easy to talk only to the people you need for a story. But that often means that your view of what's happening is limited. It's how you can easily be unfair to a group of people because you're only representing one particular group of people. For example, if you're doing a story on a teachers union's negotiations with the school district and you want to include what the average teacher thinks, it's important to talk to multiple teachers with different perspectives to see what their overall feelings are. Oftentimes, you may need to include the points of view of teachers who support the union's actions and those who don't.

Identifying the Essential Skills You Need

Being a journalist requires constant growth in your skillset. It's an industry of change, and it takes work to keep up. But even in this fast-changing world, some basic skills are essential to the work and are the foundation for everything we do.

Researching

Researching is what most people are familiar with from their school days. For journalists, it's often the very first step that we do when we're either looking for a story idea or trying to refine one. Research is all the work that's involved before we officially start reporting the story, and it's important because it helps us home in on where to start and how to use our time most efficiently.

TIP

Here are some tips for doing research specific to journalism:

» **Read, watch, and listen to what's been reported already.** Some journalists argue that there are no new stories. That's because, quite often, the stories we work on are built off of what we already know about an issue, and generally, past journalism helped us learn that. Think about how a library is a great source of information. Every story we create adds to that library of knowledge, so it's good to know what's already there and where ours fits in.

» **Lean into original documents.** There is a lot to be learned from original documents, even at this exploratory stage. Documents such as licenses, copies of forms, and so on can give you all kinds of information, and some of the best and most impactful work has come from them. For example, looking at parking ticket records can show that poor neighborhoods are being over-ticketed, or diving into public records can reveal that a city's funds are being misappropriated.

» **Do pre-reporting.** *Pre-reporting* means talking to people and sort of interviewing them but just to learn more about a topic. It's not an official interview because you may not use anything you learn. For example, you may ask someone who just

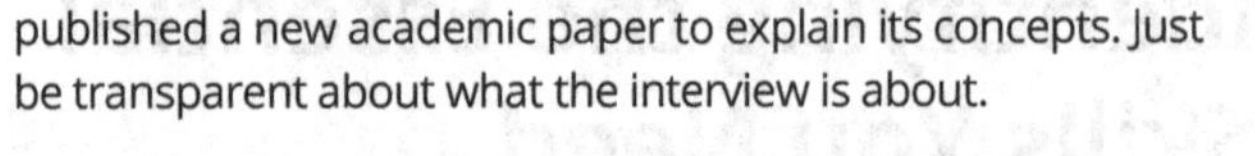
published a new academic paper to explain its concepts. Just be transparent about what the interview is about.

TIP

The connections you make during the pre-reporting process can still be extremely beneficial in the future. The key is to be open with the person you're interviewing and let them know that you're in an exploratory phase to be respectful of their time.

Reporting

The word *reporting* is often used as a catchall for everything that journalists do for a story, especially because, when we're working on a story, we are *reporters*. But when talking about skills, *reporting* means gathering information specifically for the purpose of a story.

TIP

As you're focusing on these reporting skills, here are some tips to keep in mind:

- **Get outside and go to places.** A big difference between researching and reporting is that reporting requires you to get out from behind a screen. It pushes you to physically be in the places you're going to be covering in your story so that you can experience them.
- **Talk to people and ask them questions.** Going to places also helps you meet people you would otherwise never know to seek out. When you meet them, you have the opportunity to have authentic conversations with them. You can also learn so much more about what your audience thinks that can guide even more stories. See what they care about, what they want to see in their news, what they feel isn't being reported.
- **Stay diligent.** Reporting is tough. For many of us, it can honestly be the hardest part of the process. Sometimes people don't want to talk to you. Sometimes people agree to interviews and then don't show up or stop answering your calls. There is so much that can feel beyond your control that it's easy to get frustrated. That's why it's important to know that it's all a part of the process and it's totally normal for plans to fall through.

REMEMBER

Reporting can be extremely repetitive. You often have to make similar calls, send similar emails, and ask similar questions over and over again. It also means you often have to contact the *same* person over and over again and continue to persuade and nudge people multiple times. That's part of the job, so don't feel bad for doing it. As long as you lean into your instincts on when to keep pushing and when to pivot, you'll make the right decision.

Interviewing

Interviewing is the part of journalism in which you really get to experience the beauty of human-to-human connection. It's often where you get to have the type of conversations you've seen people like Anderson Cooper and Robin Roberts have on TV.

But good interviews are a mix of talent, learned skill, and preparation. Here is how to have them:

- **Ask the right questions.** Write interview questions that are thoughtful, and then arrange them in an order that makes sense. This prep gives you a loose plan to work from, but you should still stay in the moment, truly listening to what your interviewee is saying. That way you can confidently pivot as necessary and add follow-up questions based on what your interviewee says.
- **Keep it feeling like a conversation.** The main reason why you shouldn't be stuck on your planned questions in most cases is that your conversation should feel natural. You should be open to the interview moving in new directions sometimes. And if you feel the conversation has gone too far off, gently guide it back.

TIP

Sometimes it's important to ask certain questions of an interviewee because I may need information or responses from them about specific topics. I often use time as a way to respectfully help my interviews get back on track. Saying "I know your time is precious, and I really want to make sure we have enough time to talk about X" helps me redirect us back to my planned questions when I really need to hit certain areas.

» **Be open to having multiple interviews with the same person.** Sometimes one interview just isn't enough. This fact can be especially true when there's a lot of ground to cover or when new information and angles emerge during an interview. It's okay to thank your interviewee for this conversation and simply ask if you can schedule an additional time to speak.

Fact-checking

Fact-checking ties back to our commitment to accuracy. But it's not as easy as it sounds. You can easily make mistakes that can start small and become huge. I've had my fair share of embarrassing factual errors, so I know how it feels to think to yourself: *I can't believe I didn't catch that.*

None of us is perfect, though, and some mistakes are inevitable. But there are some steps you can take to significantly reduce the risk of making mistakes that can make you seem careless:

» **Check everything and then check it twice.** It seems simple but checking your facts multiple times is just smart to do. It's so easy to miss errors the first time you go through a story. Make it a habit to do it over and over.

» **Don't be afraid to ask for help.** You don't have to be the only fact-checker for your work. You can ask a friend for help or hire someone if you're working independently.

» **Try not to fact-check the same day you write.** You can easily miss mistakes when you're tired. You can also miss them because your eyes are glossing over, reading mistakes as what you meant them to be and not what you actually wrote.

TIP

Sometimes you're finishing a story the same day it needs to be published, and you don't have an extra day for fact-checking. In that case, even a small break can help you reset from writer to fact-checker. Get up, stretch, get a snack, go for a walk — whatever takes you away from the computer for a moment and gives you the opportunity to refresh your eyes a little.

Working in a Newsroom versus Working Independently

Working in a newsroom has many benefits and is how most people envision being a journalist. It's what you see on TV shows about journalism: a big office space with people sitting around at open desks, talking on phones, gathering around screens to work on stories.

Even with the explosion of virtual and hybrid journalism work, the idea of collaboration still drives newsrooms. Journalism is driven by the philosophy that nothing is produced in a silo and that teamwork reigns supreme.

But it's not the only way to do journalism anymore. Many people have chosen to abandon newsroom life to work as independent journalists, and there are pros and cons to both.

Barriers to entry

The biggest difference between working in a newsroom and working independently is that you have to be hired on by a media company. That means that if you don't have exactly what certain jobs are hiring for at the moment, don't live in an area with many media organizations, or are newer in the industry, you could have a very tough time finding a role that matches your skills.

Many journalists who work independently now do so because they couldn't find a role in a traditional organization that was a good fit. They didn't let the lack of job opportunities stop them from doing the work they wanted to do. This road is possible for many people now that publishing can take various forms online.

Having an editor

One of the benefits of working in a newsroom is knowing you don't have to do everything alone. Having an editor that you trust is like having both a team leader to help guide your work, as well as a thought partner to help you think through your ideas.

Yet working independently doesn't mean that you can never work with an editor again. It does mean, though, that to seek the help of an editor, you would need to ask a friend for a favor or hire someone to help you when needed.

Even if you're working independently, you aren't forced to work alone. You can build systems of support for yourself. You could also pull together a group of independent journalists, and you all could help edit each other when needed.

Having editorial control

Having an editor means that the editorial control doesn't lie with you. In a traditional newsroom, when you work on a story, your editor has the final say on everything about that story — from the headline to the story content to the images used. Editors even have control over whether you can report a story at all.

This issue, of course, does not exist when working independently. It's one of the reasons cited by journalists of color, especially, who want to report on their communities but have found that when they were in traditional newsrooms, their editors didn't understand the stories they wanted to cover.

Being flexible

Flexibility is another reason that many journalists choose to work independently — setting their own schedules for how many stories they want to produce and when. However, when your goals, your editor's goals, and the goals of your media organization align, flexibility may not be a problem. The key is striking the correct balance and communicating your needs and abilities while understanding the media organization's priorities.

Working on Different Platforms

Most journalists have one (or sometimes two) media platforms that they work on. The basics of journalism are the same for everyone, but it's a good idea to identify the differences between them and what people mean when they mention these terms.

Print

As the oldest form of journalism, print — which includes newspapers and magazines — is one of the first kinds of journalism that is taught in most journalism schools. That's because even broadcast stories on TV or radio are accompanied by written stories that follow traditional newspaper-style writing.

Digital

Today, with most newspapers having an online presence and with many news organizations no longer having print publications, many people have swapped print for digital. Skill-wise, people who write for digital-only media organizations still follow print-style rules in their work. So, when you hear people say, "Oh, I'm a print reporter," it means they're primarily writers — it doesn't necessarily indicate whether that writing is ever printed or if it exists only online.

Television

TV journalists are those who work at local and national TV stations. They may do a variety of roles. For example, a multimedia journalist (MMJ) is an on-air reporter who shoots, reports, and edits their own TV *packages* (a type of story in which video is produced and edited together into a cohesive report).

Documentary video

Documentary video journalism is a bit different than the daily TV news we watch. It means journalists are working on big assignments for much longer time periods. They could be working for a major network, or often, they have their own production companies and work to pitch their documentaries to networks to air.

Radio

Broadcast radio is another one of the oldest forms of journalism, which has continued to grow and expand as technology has changed. Many of the news-specific jobs in radio are at public radio stations and networks, but many also are available at commercial radio stations as well.

Podcasting

Journalists who work in podcasting focus on long-form storytelling in audio form. They often work at podcasting-only companies or public radio stations or networks, as well as at many of the new podcast departments popping up at other large media organizations in virtually every area of journalism.

Social media

There are many roles, especially at very large media companies, in which journalists only post stories and other content on social media. For example, the "*Washington Post* TikTok guy," Dave Jorgenson, became known in the industry because he was one of the first journalists to visibly have such a high-profile job in which his role was solely to post on one social media platform. Oftentimes, social media storytelling responsibilities entail other digital duties, such as editing a website's home page.

IN THIS CHAPTER

» Understanding what journalism is and isn't

» Learning journalism standards and meeting them

» Knowing what to expect in a journalism job

Chapter 2 Defining Journalism

We see journalism often, and it's an essential part of how we live our lives — even when we aren't the ones doing it. Journalism helps us know what's happening in our world, shows us stories that connect us to humanity, and works as a tool for keeping powerful people accountable. It's helpful to get a solid grasp on journalism — what it is and what it isn't — because journalism helps us process so much of what happens.

What Journalism Is

Journalism is often simply defined as the profession of creating media, such as newspapers and broadcast TV shows. But it's more than just the act of creating the things we read, watch, and listen to for information. It's *why* and *how* we produce them that makes all the difference.

Take newsletters, for example. When a news organization creates a newsletter, it's to provide important information to an audience and it's done by vetting and including information that lives up to journalistic standards. These reasons and standards are not necessarily the same for another organization that could make a similar product. So, a newsletter from a journalism organization that shares events for local families is different than one that could be published by a toy company that is using the newsletter to push toy sales.

It may seem silly sometimes to focus on these differences, but it's important because many things that are not journalism often look the same. For example, a company blog post may read the same as a journalism article. But understanding real journalism is a skill we all should have.

The "fourth estate" and democracy

Why journalism is important boils down to its role in democracy. In school, you learned about how the U.S. Constitution outlines the three branches of government: legislative (Congress), executive (the president, vice president, and cabinet), and judicial (the Supreme Court and other federal courts). But the press is an unofficial branch, known as the "fourth estate."

Like the other checks and balances, the press is supposed to be independent — free from any interference from government agencies. It ensures that citizens get the information they deserve to know. Not all journalism falls into the category of *watchdog journalism* — a specific area in which journalists serve as monitors, or "watchdogs," by monitoring what those in government are doing.

But understanding this overall role is important because many stories still do this in some way. It also helps you understand why journalists have such a huge responsibility to report facts accurately and why they're given certain rights in order to help them do that.

Many of the popular award-winning stories that have become the most memorable in the public eye show just how essential journalism is to democracy. The Pulitzer Prize is journalism's most renowned honor, and scrolling through its list of winners is a way to see some of the best examples of the fourth estate in action.

Power and accountability

When you think about how checks and balances work, it makes sense that the press is used to keep those in power accountable. It's journalism's job to uncover the wrongdoings of people and entities in power, such as those in government and people who run major corporations.

To do this well, journalists have certain protections and rights. For example, it's why there is a White House press corps, filled with journalists from multiple news organizations, who attend briefings, travel with the president and vice president, and get the opportunity to ask questions on behalf of all of us.

As everyday citizens, most people don't get the opportunity to see what people in power are up to. So, journalists become the watchdogs. We fill in that gap. It's one of the highest honors and most essential responsibilities journalists have.

Objectivity, balance, and bias

As journalists, our job is to find ways to be fair to the people and ideas we're discussing. There is an important reason for this: In order for people to trust our work, they need to trust that we weren't intentionally trying to be unfair and biased in our reporting.

In the past, the prevalent term was *objectivity.* Journalists were taught that being objective, or showing objectivity, would prove to audiences that their work is fair and balanced, not favoring one particular side. This traditional view of objectivity involved trying to separate who you are as a journalist from who you are as a person. Common examples of this include not expressing opinions on social media, not attending rallies or protests, and not joining advocacy groups.

However, many journalists no longer use objectivity as a goal. The reasoning here is clear: It's impossible to be completely objective when subjectivity is embedded in multiple decisions that happen within the journalism process, such as deciding on the exact story angle and who to interview. These decisions are based on our individual and subjective opinions on how best to do the story. Instead of objectivity, many journalists now argue that being committed to doing all the work the story requires is a way to reach fairness.

An example of being fair would be acknowledging that people may have views you don't agree with, but you'll interview them anyway because it's what the story requires in order to do your job as a journalist.

REMEMBER

The ideas around objectivity are still changing. So, it's really important that you think about how your work as a journalist aligns with your own ethics. What are the lines in the sand that you draw for yourself? What would be a conflict for you and what wouldn't? Media organizations have their own ethical rules, but it's essential that you define your own.

THE IMPACT OF JOURNALISM'S HISTORY ON TODAY'S INDUSTRY

Today's discussion surrounding objectivity stems from the past. Journalism has been around for as long as there has been a United States. And it has continued to suffer from a lack of diversity. Now, for example, surveys show that U.S. newsrooms are less diverse than the country's overall employment base. The problem with objectivity is that it doesn't take into account that journalists from marginalized backgrounds often don't have the luxury of trying to separate their real lives from their lives as journalists for the purpose of objectivity. For example, some political journalists even say they don't vote in elections because of the appearance of objectivity. Many journalists of color will argue that staying away from elections that could drastically change their lives and the lives of those in their communities is not an option.

Journalism beats

When working in journalism organizations, roles are often divided by subject areas or *beats*. This division is not meant to be exclusionary or to force journalists to only work on one thing. The purpose is to ensure a wide range of coverage and help journalists become well versed and experienced in their individual areas.

Beat journalists can become really skilled at reporting in their areas because they're covering similar stories, and their knowledge on these topics is being added to with every new story they work on. For example, an education reporter who attends every school board meeting is the best person to cover a teachers' strike. That person knows all the background and context of what has happened in the district up to that point.

So, when it comes to deciding which beats to have, journalism leaders often lean in on what areas are most important to prioritize this kind of experience. Here are some common beats that you may find in a newsroom:

- **Politics:** The politics beat is a common one because the ins and outs of government are complicated. On both the local, state, and federal levels, it's not easy to break down, analyze, and then report on politics in a way that the everyday person can understand. So, this beat is generally a high priority for many newsrooms.
- **Education:** Education is huge in all news, but especially news on the local level because it affects how families live and work in their communities. The decisions education leaders in a city, town, or region make about their schools deserve a lot of coverage.
- **Arts, culture, and entertainment:** There is more to a city than its heaviest issues. Covering cultural issues is key to engaging communities, especially in local newsrooms, and balancing the weight of tough news coverage.
- **Crime and/or criminal justice:** Crime can be covered differently, sometimes giving audiences stories on each crime that happens throughout communities and sometimes focusing on larger stories surrounding the criminal justice system.

- **Science, health care, and the environment:** Media organizations are starting to recognize that having expertise in reporting on science is advantageous to the communities they serve. It's especially important in times of public health and climate crisis, for example, to be able to share information quickly and accurately with audiences.
- **Business and technology:** The business beat is essential to the journalism field because it often includes the economy and markets. It has continued to grow in scope as large tech companies have emerged over the past decades, with tech alone becoming a focus of many reporters.
- **Sports:** Unsurprisingly, sports is and has always been one of the most popular journalism beats. And those who work them don't seem to mind the nights and weekends because they love the adrenaline of covering live sporting events and doing features on some of the most interesting players.
- **General assignment:** Even in newsrooms that are set up with most reporters on a beat, there are still usually some reporters working as general assignment reporters, or GAs, who cover almost anything. GAs are extremely important to keeping newsrooms running because so many stories don't fit within one of a newsroom's specified beats. GAs also work on stories from any beat when its reporters are working on other stories.

TIP

For journalists hoping to become experts in a beat at some point, being a GA gives them the opportunity to report on stories that would otherwise be covered by someone else. For example, political stories usually first go to political reporters. But GAs have a shot at working on them as well. Still, there are a ton of GAs who love mixing it up and working in different areas. For them, especially, being a GA is a perfect role.

News versus opinion

Within journalism, there is a difference between what is news and what is opinion. This distinction is essential to understand because when it's on the same pages of a newspaper, for example, it's easy to mix up.

When we cover the news, it does not *ever* include our opinion. That means we even have to be careful with the words we use so as to not editorialize — adding in our perspectives — when we write or talk about news issues.

For example, if you're doing a story about someone's new job, you can't say that it's "exciting." What you *can* do is say that the person calls it an exciting opportunity and attribute how you're describing that job to them.

In an opinion piece or editorial, you can use this type of description because it's supposed to be clear to your audience that it's about what you think. But even an editorial should still have these same attributes that are present in news stories:

- Be true.
- Include facts.
- Have a strong, current angle.
- Cite its sources.

REMEMBER

Writing a strong editorial piece is a tough task. But remember that your responsibility as a journalist means being truthful, accurate, and fair. You can still do that while sharing your opinion and making an argument for it.

CITIZEN JOURNALISM

The growth and ease of citizen journalism is one of the most exciting progressions the industry has seen. Often referred to as *participatory journalism,* it's a type of grassroots journalism that is done by people, many of whom would not be considered "professional" journalists.

Citizen journalism is an evolution that has resulted from the benefits of new, online media being available and accessible to all people — giving citizens the ability to report and publish stories on the world around them without any barriers. Armed with cell phones, citizen journalists have borne witness to some of the most important moments of recent history. We've seen this everywhere — from the Black Lives Matter protests in the United States to the Arab Spring protests throughout the Middle East.

(continued)

(continued)

Here are some reasons why it's beneficial for the industry — and for democracy — for citizen journalists to be able to continue to thrive:

- **A more diverse journalism industry:** Without any traditional barriers, citizen journalism means that anyone from any background with a desire for truth in storytelling can become a journalist. It no longer means that large institutions decide what's shown and what isn't when big events occur, which is extremely important for ensuring the power to share it with everyone.
- **More manpower on the ground:** With citizen journalists, there are simply more people trying to get important work done. Citizen journalists can often get into places others can't, and the more people trying to bring light to issues, the more opportunity there is to break through.
- **Worldwide benefits:** Across the world, people are benefitting from citizen journalism. In many countries, the rights of the press are not protected. And even in the United States, the rights of the press can be ignored.

  Many citizen journalists, however, don't have the opportunity to be professionally trained. So, they may not engage in the same level of verification of information and vetting of sources that is standard in newsrooms. But they can provide firsthand, live-streamed accounts of what's happening.

  Luckily, more training is becoming available for citizen journalists to get skills training. For example, I worked with YouTube as part of its training for independent journalists around the world, and we taught them various skills-based classes.

What Journalism Isn't: Blogs, Tabloids, and Gossip

Journalism takes on many forms as it continues to evolve. But there are also many articles, posts, and other content that we consume every single day that is *not* journalism. Blogs, tabloids, and gossip media aren't the same as entertainment journalism, but they get confused for it on a daily basis. These places can cover similar topics, similar people, and similar updates, but they lack some significant standards.

Here's why blogs, tabloids, and gossip media are not journalism:

- **Lack of rigor:** When these places publish stories, they do so with none of the rigor of reported news stories. Journalism stories are different because even in entertainment, only proven facts are reported and anything that the journalist is unsure of is left out until it can be confirmed.
- **Clicks over harm:** The places that publish these types of stories also value audience clicks over the harm they can cause. For example, they often post the deaths of celebrities based on rumors and without regard for potentially harming their families and loved ones.
- **Acceptance of money:** Unlike in journalism, where payment is never accepted for tips or coverage, blogs and gossip media sites can and do accept money and other forms of payment. This process is highly unethical across journalism.

Distinguishing these websites from journalism is important, but some of these places are easier to identify than others. Here's how to spot what's real:

- **Any social media posts have associated article links.** Some creators make social media pages that are simply screenshots of images and headlines that have no actual story that you can read. These places are skimming content from real journalism stories, as well as from blogs, and sharing on social media so that their audiences can reshare. But they shouldn't be trusted or used.
- **The byline is from a person who is easily searchable.** Instead of seeing a generic byline such as "staff," most journalism articles should have the name of an actual person or at least a line at the bottom of the story that says the names of the journalists who contributed to the story (breaking news stories are often unbylined and updated by multiple people).

- **The information is found in reputable media outlets.** The information in a story should be able to be confirmed in other media. If no one else is reporting a popular breaking news story yet, it could mean that media outlets are struggling to confirm that it's true.

WARNING

Working for a tabloid-type outlet can negatively affect your reputation as a journalist. Because credibility and ethics are so important to our work, try your best to hold yourself to the same standards you would if you were working at your dream job and only accept assignments that align with those standards.

Who Sets the Standards for Truth

The goal for everything we do in journalism is to tell the truth. There are even different organizations, such as the Society of Professional Journalists (SPJ; `www.spj.org`), that help outline general standards. But the truth is not always cut-and-dried. What the truth is can actually be quite complicated at times.

So, who determines what's true? You! Ultimately, it's you as the journalist on your story who has to figure out what that means and how it applies to your work.

TIP

Here are some questions to ask yourself:

- **Are the facts I'm finding for my story true, false, or changing?** It's easy to forget that facts actually do change. What is a true fact now can be untrue later.

  For example, think about the guidance from scientists at the start of the COVID-19 pandemic. Initially, news articles said that wearing masks wasn't necessary and that washing your hands was the best way to prevent catching the virus. But when scientists learned that the virus was airborne, that fact changed. It was no longer true that we shouldn't wear masks, and previous news articles were then incorrect.
- **Am I getting my facts from the best person I can?** For the purposes of your stories, you want to ensure that

you're getting facts from people who are experts in their field. You can ask people about their opinions and personal experiences with topics, but you should be relying on the best research you can if you're adding them as fact.

If you're doing a story on climate change, for example, a scientist who is an expert in the field is the best person to provide facts. But it's okay to ask general people in the public about their personal experience with it.

- **Have I properly attributed all the facts in my story?** Every fact you use should be attributed to a person, website, or document. Proper attribution shows that the information you used is from the best sources possible.

TIP

When information is clearly attributed, your audience trusts your work more. Today's facts may become untrue next week, next month, or next year, so attribution shows that you didn't make up those facts and that you did your due diligence in trying to make your stories as truthful as possible.

Becoming a Journalist

Although it's not the only way to become a journalist, getting a full-time journalism job, internship, or fellowship is an involved process. In the following sections, I cover what to expect at each step.

Applying for a job

Showing your clips is an important part of most application processes. So, be sure to have a strong portfolio that you can link to whenever you want to apply for a job.

Cover letters often matter in journalism jobs. That's because, although the stories in your portfolio are likely highly edited, your cover letter probably is not. Hiring managers sometimes believe that a cover letter can show how you truly write, so it can be a benefit to you to write a great one.

Interviewing

It's not uncommon to have at least two rounds of interviews, and although you can be prepared for the normal situational questions, there are also some other areas to study:

- » An analysis of the media organization's current coverage
- » Your ideas for how your stories would fit in there
- » An overall understanding of the current news landscape

Taking writing and editing tests

One thing that can be surprising about applying for journalism jobs: There is almost always some type of extensive writing and editing test involved. These tests can take multiple hours and ask you to do multiple aspects of the role you'd be performing. Skills you could be tested on include the following:

- » Coming up with story ideas
- » Writing your own stories
- » Editing stories already written
- » Writing headlines
- » Creating social media posts
- » Taking tests (for business internships)
- » Writing code (for interactive roles)

TIP

Because these tests are so lengthy, there has been a greater push in the industry to get employers to pay interviewees for their time. Many employers still don't pay applicants, but more and more are starting to include payments or giving these tests only to applicants in the final rounds of interviewing. These changes show that a company values applicants' time and the investment they're making in the process.

What to Expect in a Journalism Job

After you get hired into a journalism role and start in a newsroom for the first time, there is a lot that could be happening: TVs or radios everywhere playing the news, people gathered at desks to meet, and phones ringing. So, it's helpful to know some of what to expect.

The structure of a newsroom

No two organizations are the same, but it can be helpful to know a little bit about newsroom hierarchy and who may be who:

- **Top-level editors:** At the top of a newsroom's editorial side are editors who oversee the overall editorial direction. Depending on the size of the organization, these journalists will have titles such as *editor-in-chief* and *executive editor.*
- **Middle-managing editors:** Midsize to large journalism organizations will likely have a level of editors who are more hands-on but are likely not editing many stories if any at all. They help keep the newsroom ticking by running meetings, checking metrics, and doing more daily work. They may have the title of *managing editor* or *deputy editor.*
- **The desks:** Reporters as well as other roles such as producers are often grouped in departments or desks, each with its own editor or set of editors to edit its stories.

With this hierarchy, there are a lot of meetings and check-ins to keep everyone on the same page:

- **Editors' meetings:** These meetings are held so that all editors can talk about what stories their reporters are working on. In newsrooms that produce a lot of stories every day, these meetings could be held every day or multiple times a day.

» **Desk or department meetings:** Editors meet with their own reporters to keep everyone on track, share updates, and brainstorm new ideas.

» **All-hands or all-staff meetings:** These meetings may not be held as often, but they're a good way to learn what the entire organization is focused on and get updates from top-level editors.

The business goals of a media business

Journalists at media organizations don't often understand — or discuss — the business part of where they work until they learn about problems through layoffs or other issues. Knowing about the business of media may not be your primary goal, but here are some parts to keep in mind:

» **The business side is separate from the editorial side.** In journalism, these sides must remain separate. That means that journalists' work is not influenced by things like the need to impress advertisers or the preferences of the chief executive officer (CEO).

» **Every media business has a different business model.** Most for-profit media businesses get their revenue from some mix of subscriptions and advertisements, whereas most nonprofit media organizations rely mostly on individual donations, grants, sponsorships, and large philanthropic giving.

» **Audience views drive sponsorship and advertisement.** You should never make editorial decisions based on what the business side of an organization wants. But you *should* understand how advertisement and sponsorship work — and how what you do supports that when you do it well. When something you publish becomes popular, views or listens (depending on the platform) increase, and people on the business side use those numbers to raise money from sponsors and advertisers.

IN THIS CHAPTER

» Understanding media literacy

» Thinking about how media affects you

» Identifying "fake news"

Chapter 3 Media Literacy: What It Is and Why It Matters

The internet is a vast repository of information. There is so much information to be found, and it's all at our fingertips. But that comes with an even larger problem: How do we know what to trust and what not to? Distinguishing this difference has become harder than ever.

Understanding what information actually is, where it comes from, and who has created it is no longer an easy act. Because it is easy to create websites, anyone can build what looks like a news site. With the advent of self-publishing, anyone can publish a book without editors and without any peer review. And, with social media, anyone can create a persona of an expert without the training, credentials, and experience to share advice or information.

That's where media literacy — the ability to look at and analyze all the media we take in as consumers — comes in. This teaching of critical thinking is also helpful to journalists because it's essential for journalists to understand how their audiences understand the work they produce. It also can guide journalists in creating work that battles the false information people see every day.

Understanding Media Literacy

Media literacy as a field of study is not new, but interest in it has grown exponentially in the 21st century as technological advances have given us access to media 24/7. So much information is coming at us from all directions, and we need a little guidance to think critically about it. Media includes everything written and published online and in print, but it also includes videos and art. The underlying belief behind media literacy is that there's a relationship that we have with media, and in order to understand that relationship, we have to examine what messages they're telling us.

According to the National Association for Media Literacy Education (NAMLE), all people should be actively interrogating all the media they consume. NAMLE suggests that people ask questions within the following three areas:

- **Authors and audiences:** These questions focus on who made the media and why, such as:
  - Who was included in making the media and who was not?
  - When was the media made and why?
  - Who paid for and/or makes money from the media?
- **Messages and meanings:** This area of analysis involves the actual content and its format. Examples of these questions include:
  - What messages are clear and what messages are implied?
  - What is left out altogether?
  - How is the format itself a communication tool, and what does that say to me?

Some people and organizations are really great at making media that *looks* like it's something that it's not in order to intentionally trick people. For example, if a political ad disguised as a fake newspaper is delivered to people's homes, but it's printed like a newspaper, has headlines and photos like a newspaper, and is written in the tone that newspaper articles often use, it's very easy for people to mistake it as a newspaper. This is an intentional deception — one that may work very well on someone who is not very media literate.

- **Reflections and evaluations:** Questions in this area are about people's own interpretations of the media and its credibility:
  - How am I interpreting the media, and how might others interpret it differently?
  - Is there a productive way to respond to how the media makes me feel?
  - How do I know the sources used are credible?

Every single piece of media has a message, every single author of a media product has a purpose, and credibility has to be earned and kept, so it's okay to be cautious. There is an old journalism adage that says: "If your mother says she loves you, get another source." It basically means that you should double-check *everyone*, and it encourages new journalists to be skeptical of information so that they don't fall for untruths. But let's use this adage for an exercise, using your knowledge of how to interrogate media messages.

For example, say it's your birthday, and your mother posts a message on your Facebook page saying that she loves you. Here are some ways to think about that message:

- It's posted by your mother, for the purpose of wishing you a happy birthday.
- Your mother doesn't really get any benefit from this message other than spreading well wishes, unless there is a reason she would want people specifically on Facebook to know.

- » Your mother's feelings seem credible because they match up with how she speaks to you and treats you.
- » As you reflect on your own feelings, you're definitely biased in how you see and have experienced your mother.

The exact same words would be unbelievable coming from some people. There could be many reasons why someone would want to be misleading in a Facebook post. So, you can see how the authorship, purpose, credibility, and so on naturally come into play when analyzing common messages. However, when you're taking in the large amount of information you receive on a daily basis, you have to train your mind to think through it all.

REMEMBER

Media literacy extends past journalism stories. But it's helpful to think through these questions for all types of media because it helps you learn how to be thoughtful in your analysis. Media literacy is a muscle that you're building up so it becomes second nature.

Recognizing How Media Affects You

Analyzing media is essential because it involves many of our rights as citizens who are part of a democracy. In the United States, as well as in other countries that champion free speech, media is used to share information that is pertinent to how people live their daily lives. So, it's extremely important that it's well understood.

People who may not see the value in media literacy may see media only for its entertainment value or for its ability to help people communicate with each other, like in the form of social media. But it has significant consequences for the decisions we make, how we view the world, and how we navigate life as citizens.

REMEMBER

We may be journalists, but we're also citizens. It's important to think through how we use media ourselves to better understand how others may also use it.

Your right to be informed

You have a right, as a citizen of where you live, to be informed and knowledgeable about what's going on. It isn't an exaggeration to express that this right governs how you move through your life.

Here are just some examples of ways that being informed affects people:

- **Voting:** Many people express that one of their biggest concerns when there is a lack of media literacy is that it affects people's ability to have what they need when they go to vote for their elected officials.
- **Local policies:** Local policies, such as tax law, affect people more than they seem to realize. It's pertinent that people are informed about what the local policies are, any changes that are occurring to those policies, and opportunities to share their thoughts and opinions on them.
- **Agencies and services:** Park services, garbage pickup, construction on infrastructure, and other "small" things that people utilize every day are not so small when you truly think about them. People need to be informed about what's happening with these agencies and services.

To make an informed decision, you have to first be able to trust that the information you're basing it on is true. For example, when I vote for judges in my local county and state, I use guides that tell me about their records, their history, and their experience. I'm trusting that this information is correct so I can then decide which judges I would like to see on the bench as a citizen.

Your right to find the information you seek

It's also your right to be able to find information when you're looking for it. This can be particularly difficult because online searches can produce many results that aren't true or helpful.

So, as you examine media that everyone has access to, here are some places to look for answers:

- **Credible news:** The news is often your first stop as media consumers for information. But you want to ensure that you're looking at media organizations that you trust and that have proven their credibility.

  TIP

  If you're unsure if what you're seeing on the news is accurate and you need a quick check, find a second source. Even credible places can get things wrong if they're working to quickly get information out, so pause, take a moment, and find an additional source to verify what you're reading, seeing, or hearing. If it's true, other news media will also be reporting on it.
- **Public records:** Many people don't realize that you don't have to be a journalist to submit public records requests from government agencies. The Freedom of Information Act (FOIA) gives everyone in the United States this right. Every agency has its own rules and processes for such requests, though. Simply search the web for "public information request" or search for an agency's public information office or officer.
- **Public meetings:** Anyone can attend a public meeting, but meetings are often held during the day when many people are working. Most municipal offices keep records of the minutes from these meetings, and now, after many meetings moved online during COVID-19, they're often live-streamed and their recordings are stored.

Your right as a citizen to monitor those in power

When you think about civics and the rights of citizenship, media literacy plays a huge role. Journalists have the duty to monitor those in power, but all citizens have that right, too. And in order to do so, they need access to information.

This is why media literacy has also become a large part of general literacy, especially in schools. Here are some ways that media, as a form of communication, supports this work:

» **Contacting officials:** Letting government officials know what you think is essential. Traditionally, letters were the only way to reach them. But now, with the magic of email and social media, messages can be sent quickly. You can even use email templates created for various causes if you're not quite sure what to say or how to say it.

» **Organizing protests and rallies:** Getting people together for a common cause can be difficult, but strong media messaging — especially on social media — can help. With many youth-led initiatives, young people have harnessed the power of social media to make it happen.

» **Following lawmakers' records:** To access legislators voting records, for example, you can use government websites such as `www.senate.gov`, `www.house.gov`, and `www.congress.gov`. And, if you have a special interest, you can use curated scorecards from places such as the American Federation of Labor and Congress of Industrial Organizations, better known as the AFL-CIO. Its legislative scorecard is based on issues important to its mission, such as workplace safety, Social Security, and Medicare.

TIP

Even if you think your elected officials aren't paying attention to what their constituents are saying on social media, it's likely that their staff members are. Use it to your advantage by making smart and strong statements that are clear and professional.

Identifying Fake News

The term *fake news* is one that, today, some people loosely throw around, often when there is news they believe shouldn't be believed or trusted. For example, a celebrity or other figure in the public eye may say that a story that is about them is "fake news" simply because they don't like it and want people to disregard it.

However, there *is* such a thing as fake news — news that is not true, is not real, and may even be created specifically to mislead audiences.

Seeing where fake news crops up

Fake news shows up in the following forms:

- **"Experts" who are not experts:** Journalists must properly vet the experts they use. When you amplify voices sharing false information, the effect can be large.
- **"Journalists" who don't care about accuracy:** Anyone can call themselves a journalist today, and that includes people who don't want to commit to the level of accuracy required for the job. This could include a range of people — from those who haven't yet learned the skill to those who don't value fact-checking and don't see a problem with spreading incorrect information.
- **"News" that isn't news:** So much media looks like it's journalism, but it simply isn't, and so many media outlets have no commitment to journalistic standards. But these sources often look just like other media outlets, so audiences must examine them to figure out if they're real or fake.

There are also some areas in which fake news appears more than others. Here are some ways it can show up in what people consume:

- **In breaking news:** *Breaking news* is news that's reported rapidly, right as it's happening and immediately after. It's tough to get right because facts can actually change as more information is learned. Even the best breaking news reporters can fall into a trap of hastily reporting incorrect information if they aren't careful.
- **In politics:** Politics is often a huge area for fake news because the stakes of political elections are so high. Even if candidates and their campaigns are committed to truth-telling, supporters can help spread untruths — and they do so very quickly.
- **In science:** Science, something many people think is cut-and-dried in the area of facts, can be controversial and confusing when people are affected by it and desperate for answers. For example, these untruths often appear when talking about the drastic effects of climate change or when people want a new suggested medical treatment to be a miracle save.

REMEMBER

At the start of the COVID-19 pandemic, as people were desperate for anything they thought could help save them and their loved ones, many unhealthy "treatments" were touted as miracle drugs. This desperation helped fuel the growth of fake science and fake news to boot.

- **In crime:** People love true crime, and they love to find what they think is a solution to unsolved cases. This desire to be a part of the story has led to many people seeing themselves as amateur detectives. They may spread their own theories — even accusing innocent people in the process — even though doing so can be detrimental to the very cases they want to help.

Distinguishing among the different types of fake news

Although many of these untruths have similar consequences, intent comes into play in how they're classified. Many people use the terms *misinformation, disinformation,* and *malinformation* interchangeably, but they mean very different things, and identifying what those differences are can help with thinking through how people can combat them.

Misinformation

Misinformation is simply information that is factually incorrect. But the key to understanding misinformation is that it isn't intentional. Misinformation could stem from people just being wrong about something and not actually having the expertise to provide the right information.

When people are desperate for answers to a pressing problem, they're willing to believe anything that seems as if it could be exactly what they're looking for — even if it's untrue.

Here are some examples of misinformation:

- A video on TikTok spreading an unverified claim about using a drug for a different purpose
- A screenshot of a news article without context and without the article text to explain what the story is about

- A blog post about a crime that happened, including the author's own theories and ideas not in any official file
- A parody or satire social media account about a celebrity that doesn't intend to mislead people but is mistaken as true

Disinformation

Unlike misinformation, *disinformation* is not just factually incorrect but is also created with the intent to deceive people. When people say something is fake news, disinformation is most often what they're referring to — something that was made for the purpose of spreading incorrect information.

Here are some examples of the types of disinformation that appear quite often:

- An article written by a fake news site that spreads untrue information about a trending issue everyone is talking about
- A social media account pretending to be a celebrity or other famous person that starts a rumor
- A *deepfake* political video on YouTube, in which the creator has used technology to make someone appear to be saying something they never said

Malinformation

Malinformation can be a bit challenging to notice. It's defined as information that starts as true but is then used to cause harm. The info could be exaggerated, misconstrued, or misrepresented. It can be tricky to notice.

Here are some examples of how malinformation can come into play:

- A news story that has an error saying someone is accused of a crime, and now that error is being spread maliciously, even though it has been corrected

- A screenshot of a news article posted on Instagram with untrue information in the caption
- Real footage of an event shared and claimed to be from a different event

WARNING

Although misinformation, disinformation, and malinformation are different, scholars who study them stress that information can move from category to category. Information that was simply untrue can then be used to intentionally deceive people, even after it's proven wrong.

Distinguishing what's true from what's false

Deciphering what's true and not can be difficult. And sometimes, in the moment, you find a fact that you're struggling with but that you want to figure out quickly. If you find yourself in this situation, break it down to these three quick questions before you share it:

- **Is it possible?** Does it make sense that this information is true? Some things seem too outlandish to be possible because they aren't.
- **Is it changing?** Was something true that could no longer be true? Facts change so think about how this may possibly be one of those facts.
- **Is it harmful?** If sharing information may cause harm, it doesn't help anyone to share it prematurely. You don't want to contribute to any harm.

TIP

People who intentionally create fake news to deceive people are quite good at it. They know what can affect people's emotions and what would make people want to share that information immediately. Slowing down and pausing instead of instinctively sharing a post or article without thinking sometimes gives you the few moments you need to naturally notice if something is fishy about it.

2 Understanding the Reporting Process

IN THIS PART . . .

Dive into how to be a reporter by figuring out what is newsworthy and how that is determined.

Learn how to find sources for a story and the various categories they fall in.

Explore interviewing, with a special emphasis on what happens before, during, and after an interview.

Get a grasp on the meticulous fact-checking process, and figure out how to make sure your numbers are always accurate in your stories.

IN THIS CHAPTER

» Understanding story types

» Using new, emerging forms of storytelling

Chapter 4 Identifying Different Types of Stories

Although the basics of journalism don't change much, how we share our reporting does. And many different types of stories can result from it. Many media organizations even have their own standardized story formats. But there are still some overall basic categories that stories often fall into.

In this chapter, I walk you through the tried-and-true types of journalism stories, from breaking news to obituaries and more. I also introduce you to emerging digital formats, so you're prepared to write stories, no matter the format.

Looking at the Traditional Story Types

There are some types of traditional news stories that every journalists should know. These stories serve the public in different ways, and their formats reflect the best way to do just that.

Breaking news

Breaking news is what people often envision when they think about journalism: reporters running around to the scene of a big event. And it's still one of the most important things journalists do, because when big events happen, it's journalists' duty to inform the public of what's going on.

Keep in mind the following tips when writing breaking news stories:

- **Structure:** The structure of a breaking news story is always in what is called the *inverted pyramid.* That means that the most important facts are at the top of the story. The lesser the fact, the lower it goes. (You may add in a paragraph in which you outline the chronological order of how something occurred, but where the paragraph goes in this structure still depends on the importance of those facts.)

  Breaking news stories start with a straight news lead — a one-sentence paragraph that tells as many facts as possible in the least amount of words (who, what, when, where, why, and how).

  In this book, I use the spelling *lead,* but take note that many people also spell it as *lede* and might use these words interchangeably as they write. It's not uncommon to see people use both spellings.

  If breaking news stories are in print (a newspaper or website), the length should be short — sometimes just a couple hundred words — so people can read them quickly. They may get longer as reporters gather more information, but they generally are still around 500 words or less. If breaking news stories are on broadcast TV or radio, they may be as short as less than a minute.

Because breaking news stories are so short, there isn't any fluff added to make sentences flow. The flow comes from lining up the facts logically.

- **Voice and tone:** In all mediums, the writing of a breaking news story is straightforward. Sentences are concise and clear.
- **Details:** Breaking news stories are detail driven. Every sentence is likely packed with facts.

Breaking news is often written quickly, and it's easy to feel rushed. But take the extra minutes you need to ensure that your facts are correct and that they make sense to you.

In addition to writing, there are also some things to consider while reporting:

- **Who to talk to:** Try to talk to everyone you can, with the hope of getting as close to those involved with the event as possible. You want to interview people who were there.
- **What perspectives to include:** In breaking news, you'll want to include the perspectives of witnesses, people involved in the event, and officials such as representatives from the police or fire departments, city officials, and so on.
- **What other info to gather:** In addition to getting all the facts you can from the events themselves, you'll want to also try to find facts that can give the audience context of the event. For example, if you're covering a tornado, find out the most recent data about tornado incidents in the area to add.

When you're in a newsroom, breaking news is a group activity. Even if you're the reporter on a breaking news story, you can ask for help. For example, a colleague can help find the additional tornado data for you while you cover the event on the ground.

Meetings and events

Covering meetings and events can be tricky because newer reporters often struggle to find out what the actual news is when it's time to write the story.

TIP

In these stories, the news is *what happened* at the event and never that the event happened.

For example, if covering a city council meeting, the news is not that there was a meeting when there is a planned meeting every month. The news could be that the council cut funding to something, or that it raised taxes, or even that arguments ensued. But it should never simply be that the meeting happened.

TIP

Keep in mind the following tips when writing stories on meetings and events:

- **Structure:** The structure of these stories should focus on what happened in order of importance. Starting this type of story really leans in on that focus. The story's lead could be a straight-news lead that highlights the most important thing that happened, or it could be a *summary lead,* which summarizes multiple things that happened in a single sentence.

  The length of these stories can vary, depending on what happened, but they shouldn't be excessively long.

  The flow of the story is dictated by how much happened that the audience would care about.

- **Voice and tone:** These stories, because they're informational, should be clear and concise and shouldn't use flowery language, unless it's appropriate for the event. For example, it would be more acceptable to use wordy language to describe art in a story about a gallery opening, but using that tone in a story about a city council budget meeting wouldn't work.
- **Details:** Extra details are helpful, especially if the event is a visual one, such as a parade or a performance. Adding extra details that describe the scene can help audiences picture what happened as they read or hear your story if it's not on TV.

Additional reporting considerations for meetings and events include the following:

- **Who to talk to:** You want to talk to as many people who are there as possible.
- **What perspectives to include:** If people have different thoughts, experiences, or backgrounds, try to represent that in your story.
- **What other info to gather:** Additional information may need to be added to give context to past meetings, especially in the case of governmental meetings.

REMEMBER

The lead sets the focus of your story. It should never simply say that an event or meeting occurred.

Enterprise stories

Enterprise stories further a conversation past what can be covered in a short story that is based on just one event or one occurrence. The name can be confusing because it may make you think that it refers to business reporting specifically, but that's not the case.

Enterprise stories are a category of stories that are more in-depth than same-day stories. They take a lot more time because they focus on why and how things happen. They often look at trends, rely on data and research, and sometimes come from scoops or tips that a journalist uncovers.

How an enterprise story can grow from breaking news is a great illustration of this kind of difference. For example, a hurricane that has ravaged a town is breaking news. But an enterprise story could examine how the town's buildings weren't properly built or whether the local government acted quickly enough to give residents time to evacuate.

TIP

Keep in mind the following tips when writing enterprise stories:

- **Structure:** The structure of enterprise stories can vary, taking on elements you'd see in breaking news and in features, depending on the media outlet's preference and style. These stories could have more of a straight-news lead or an anecdotal lead. These stories are generally longer, similar to feature-length stories. It may be common to see helpful subheadings throughout an enterprise story to help with its flow.

- **Voice and tone:** These stories are seen as "hard" news and should generally have a serious tone.
- **Details:** You should add many relevant details, using the opportunity to describe important processes, scenes, and so on whenever necessary.

When you're reporting these stories, give yourself time to work on them, often over a long period of time. Sometimes your editor will give you the space to set your own deadlines early on in the project until it starts to shape up. But sometimes, your overall time is more constrained, and in that case, it's important to ask for the time you need. Think about:

- **Who to talk to:** Enterprise stories require a long list of interviewees, even if only some of them end up in your final story.
- **What perspectives to include:** There is no magic number but the shortest of enterprise stories may have at least three to five voices included.
- **What other info to gather:** Because enterprise stories are built on breaking news stories and other shorter stories, it's important to get a good grasp on what has happened if it's not a beat that you've been covering.

REMEMBER

The difference between breaking news and enterprise news is time. So, make sure that your story shows that distinction. It should never feel rushed or as though it's lacking key information.

Investigative work

Investigative reporting is one of the main ways journalists hold people and organizations in power accountable. This aspect is what distinguishes investigative work from general features or enterprise stories, which it may look like format-wise.

Keep in mind the following tips when writing investigative stories:

- **Structure:** Long investigative projects often become either one long-form story or a series of several stories. Highlighting the impact of how problems and issues affect real people is important, so anecdotes are generally included. These anecdotes are used to support the hard data that drives the investigation.
- **Voice and tone:** The stories are serious and the writing reflects that, with clear explanations of the issue.
- **Details:** The long length of these stories creates room to allow many details to help drive home the importance of the issue being investigated. The details include a lot of data gathered via records or primary sources that have been meticulously corroborated.

Reporting investigative stories is a specialized type of reporting. It can take many years to hone these skills. But there are some tips that can help you dive deeper into your reporting than you would for other stories:

- **Who to talk to:** Talk to far more people than you think you need to. This helps you cross every T and dot every I.
- **What perspectives to include:** When it comes to the final product, you can't possibly include every voice. But you want to include enough perspectives to show the audience how many different people are affected by the issue.
- **What other info to gather:** Find data and original documents, such as those acquired by sending public information requests.

Whenever you're writing about someone or some entity — especially if the story or someone quoted in it is accusing them of doing something — always reach out to them for an interview and include whether they responded. Here are some sample responses to include if they don't agree to be interviewed:

- **If they send a statement:** "The [entity name] said in a statement. . . ."

» **If they decline an interview:** "The [entity name] declined a request for interview" or "The [entity name] declined to be interviewed."

» **If they don't respond at all:** "The [entity name] did not respond to a request for interview."

Features and profiles

Think of feature stories and profiles of interesting people as stories that are especially interesting for audiences because they highlight the uniqueness of a person, place, group, or organization. The goal with feature stories and profiles is to show an up-close-and-personal look at the subject of the story.

TIP

Keep in mind the following tips when writing features and profiles:

» **Structure:** Whereas breaking news follows the inverted pyramid style of conveying facts in order of importance or chronology, features and profiles convey information in more of a creative narrative, grouping similar information and facts together, regardless of chronology. They often start with an *anecdotal lead* (a lead that tells a story about a person or group of people). From there, the structure often changes.

  The length of features can also be much longer. This is true for written features, such as those in newspapers and magazines, as well as in features in other forms, such as audio features on the radio and video features on TV.

  Features and profiles often aim to be easy to read so they should flow well with tons of detail and scene-setting information.

» **Voice and tone:** Features and profiles may also be more conversational and have room for a more creative voice than other types of stories.

» **Details:** The more details, the better.

TIP

Because feature structures can be so creative, you can increase your skill in this area by dissecting the structure of the features you love. Pay attention to the lengths of various sections with extra attention to how they start.

When reporting features and profiles, you can easily let your guard down and forget the basic tenets of journalism, but here are some things to keep in mind:

- **Who to talk to:** Talk to many, many people — not just those who you're featuring. Talking to other people confirms that what the subject of your story is telling you is true.
- **What perspectives to include:** Because these stories aren't marketing or advertising, you want to show multiple perspectives in your feature. For example, if you're featuring a store that's doing an innovative practice to give back to its community, talk to people all around the community about their perspectives, as well as those who work at or represent the store, such as the store owner, employees, and repeat customers.
- **What other info to gather:** The additional info required for a feature varies depending on the story, but dig deep and look for any additional facts that support why this feature is important.

WARNING

Be careful not to do PR for the person or organization. Remember to still do your due diligence of finding and sharing all the information about them to paint a full picture, not just a rosy one.

Obituaries

Writing obituaries may seem like a somber task, but it's an important and respected responsibility in a newsroom. Obits for prominent people are often mostly prewritten, researched, and sourced well in advance so that in the case of death, most of it is already prepared.

TIP

Keep in mind the following tips when writing obituaries:

- **Structure:** The structure of obits often mirrors profiles, except they have a more standard start. They always start with information about why the person is a prominent figure and then explain that they died and at what age. The top also explains who confirmed the death and the cause, if it's known. After the major details at the top, they flow like a profile, highlighting people's lives and major accomplishments. The length of an obit depends on the person, so it can vary greatly.
- **Voice and tone:** There is room to be light and add in quotes that share how a person was admired and loved. For more controversial figures, the tone in an obit may be a little more serious and straightforward to avoid seeming as if the writer is making any judgments.
- **Details:** Whenever possible, seek lots of details and stories from loved ones that can show more about a person.

Reporting for obits mirrors reporting for profile stories:

- **Who to talk to:** Talk to many people who knew the person.
- **What perspectives to include:** Include the voices of people who knew the person in different ways — for example, family, friends, and professional colleagues.
- **What other info to gather:** Be sure to include any major accomplishments and awards.

Editorials

Editorials are different from news because they involve the opinion of the journalist or contributors writing them. They can take many forms:

- **Opinion pieces:** Newspaper stories that are trying to persuade you of something
- **Columns:** Periodic editorials written by the same author that often talk about a similar subject every time they're published

» **Reviews:** Stories that give the journalists' opinions, often about things such as movies, TV shows, restaurants, and more

There is no one editorial structure; most media organizations create their own.

TIP

Before pitching an editorial, look at that particular place's structure, tone, and voice for the type of editorial you'd like to do. Analyze it and formulate your pitch specifically for it.

WARNING

It's a misconception that an editorial doesn't need to be reported at all — that's simply not the case. Similar to how you would research an essay, you're backing up your thesis with facts.

When reporting any story that shares an opinion, you must still:

» Find verified sources of information, data, and facts.

» Consider perspectives you may not have and find a way to learn more about them.

» Fact-check your own claims before publishing.

TIP

Think of editorial writing as not just sharing an opinion but sharing an *informed* opinion.

Exploring Emerging Digital Forms

Because newsrooms are no longer forced into print, TV, and radio formats alone, they take advantage of their websites to create and try new story formats that make sense for a world in which information is searched for online. Many new journalism organizations were created to live online only and do award-winning work while being known for creating innovative digital stories.

Aggregated stories

One of the most popular forms you'll see on news websites is *aggregation* (the practice of pulling from other journalists' reported stories to create your own instead of talking to sources directly).

Of course, if there are errors in the original reporting you're pulling from, you're repeating those mistakes, so some places still don't publish aggregated stories or keep them for "soft" news topics only. Aggregation is why a mistake in entertainment reporting can spread so quickly — many entertainment and culture-based news sites rely heavily on aggregation, and a single rumor can accidentally be reported in many places before anyone fact-checks and corrects it.

Because of this issue, you'll want to be very careful when creating aggregated stories. Only use news sources you've vetted.

The structure and tone of these stories vary, but they're often shorter in length because they're made for easy consumption by audiences. The attribution to other sites should also be very clear and should be prominent in appearance.

Some media organizations require journalists to create many aggregated stories per day, so it can be easy to fall into a process of rushing. But remember to slow down and check as much as you can for accuracy.

Listicles

A *listicle* is a numbered list that usually explains the what, why, how, and even sometimes the when or where. It's a newer form of story that's easy to consume and extremely shareable.

Here are some examples of listicles:

- 7 Ways to Lower Your Utility Bills
- 5 Reasons Why Climate Change Is Changing How We Live
- 10 Places to Travel This Summer

The list follows a brief introduction of the story. Its tone is usually conversational, keeping the audience in mind.

Explainers

An *explainer* is just as it sounds: a type of story that has the goal of explaining a complicated idea or phenomenon. Explainers can be found in almost every form, so their structure varies greatly. But explainers that are in the form of videos or Q&As are easy to digest, so they're frequently used.

The key to explainers is to be as conversational as possible in tone and to ensure that they're visually easy to scan, if in written form. Explainers often have many headings and subheads, bolding, and short sentences.

TIP

Explainers can also be in the form of other stories, such as listicles, so think of an explainer as a type of content that can easily be paired with other formats.

Interactive stories

Interactive stories live on the internet in a form that would not be possible to replicate in print, on TV, or on the radio. They often have multimedia elements and give the reader the choice to click, explore, or participate in other ways to get more information.

Some common features that you may find in these stories are:

- Maps and charts that you can click on or scroll through
- Photo galleries
- Embedded videos

IN THIS CHAPTER

» Looking at what makes a story news

» Understanding how newsroom decisions are made

» Working through disagreements

Chapter 5 Determining What's Newsworthy

Despite what some people think, not everything is newsworthy — depending on the journalism organization and its audience. There is so much going on at all times, but not everything can make the pages of a magazine or appear in a TV news program. So, journalists use a list of criteria to help them decide what they should cover.

Leaning into this criteria also helps early journalists correct one of their most common errors: mistaking an issue or a topic for a story. Unfortunately, most of what new journalists pitch as stories are not actually stories. They may be really interesting issues, but they aren't quite developed into the detail they need to be a story angle.

One of my journalism professors explained it to us like this: Your story angle is just a single blade of grass, but when your story is too wide and undefined, you're trying to cover the whole lawn.

So, as a student, I would go back to the list of criteria that make a story newsworthy and try to home in on what the story could be within this wide topic I wanted to explore. Chances are, there was a story there, but I needed to find the newsworthiness in order to take it from something to discuss to something I could actually report.

In this chapter, I guide you through how journalists choose story ideas and how the different standards of newsworthiness come into play. I also help you understand the newsroom hierarchy in who makes these decisions and offer advice on how you can get your ideas approved.

Standards for Approving a Story Idea

In a traditional newsroom, the story idea process can be a pretty collaborative one. Your editor can help you talk through your story idea and refine it, but so can others in your newsroom. Working together in this way is beneficial because when you're thinking about what's newsworthy to you, you should also be thinking about what's newsworthy to others. You want to have an expanded view of what's interesting and appeals to multiple people of different backgrounds and experiences, all while keeping your audience in mind.

Because of this idea, criteria or standards for newsworthiness can be helpful because they push you to truly think about what you're proposing and challenge you to define exactly what angle you're taking.

In the following sections, I fill you in on some of the standards journalists think about when identifying whether a story is newsworthy.

The impact of the idea or event

If an idea or event has a huge impact, it's usually news. That's because audiences need to know what's happening around them.

Reporting on stories that affect people's lives is our responsibility, so that usually pushes a story idea to the top of the list of a newsroom's priorities.

Impact is sometimes defined as impacting a large number of people — for example, if an issue affects many residents in a city. However, great impact should also make a story a priority if it's about a large percentage of a smaller community. Such stories are often underreported because they're easy to miss and difficult to find.

Many award-winning stories impact a large percentage of marginalized communities, communities that are not reported on as much, and stories that are overlooked. When journalists first come up with these story ideas, they sometimes have to prove that there is considerable impact. If your editor challenges your story idea, don't be discouraged! Do some pre-reporting to find some data, facts, or other tips to help you make a compelling case for their importance.

The proximity of the occurrence to the news audience

Proximity is a bit of a clearer metric of newsworthiness: If something happens and it's near or within the geographic area that you cover, then it can be newsy enough to report on. However, proximity alone generally isn't enough. Proximity can help define the angle you'll take, and it can also be an easy way to eliminate angles or ideas altogether.

For example, this standard is extremely helpful in local news. If you're hoping to do a profile on someone, they usually have to have a connection to that place — it's their hometown, they worked there, they're holding an event there, they're an author who wrote about the place, and so on. But there has to be a connection; otherwise, the story doesn't make sense for that particular audience.

If you're not sure if a certain story has a connection to a place, simply ask the person you're considering interviewing (or if the story is being pitched to you, ask the publicist). If there's no proximity to the story when there needs to be, don't feel bad about not pursuing it. It doesn't mean it's not a good story. It just means it's not a good story for *you.*

The timeliness of the idea

There is a saying that today's news is old tomorrow, and that's because there's no point in doing a story that gives the same information that people in your audience already know. Journalists' goal is to do the opposite: to inform. So, doing a story that doesn't feel recent won't serve that purpose.

However, there are ways to take an idea that feels stale and think of a fresh angle. Your story can:

» **Advance the conversation.** Are there more details that are now available that make the story much more detailed than when news first broke? If so, it may be worth doing a story, especially if the story corrects incorrect information or fills in important gaps.

  For example, let's say you don't report on a fire that happened yesterday at an apartment building. It's too late to do a story that simply mentions the details that everyone had yesterday. But, if today, the fire department held a press conference and released the cause of the fire, that's a reason to do a story, even if you didn't cover it yesterday.

» **Look deeper into the why of the issue.** Looking into why something happened generally can't happen immediately. It comes a bit later. So, it's normal for this story to come after the initial stories. This type is often called an enterprise story (see Chapter 4) because it discusses a bigger issue — one that caused the incident.

  In the fire example, if it's determined that the fire was caused by negligence on the part of the building's owner, you may look into:

  - Whether there are any complaints against the owner
  - What city or state policies could have protected tenants
  - What the laws are regarding this type of negligence

» **Add new perspectives.** Sometimes, especially when news first breaks, stories will only have interviews from people who could be found and talked to quickly. This is totally normal because time is of the essence. So, focusing on other voices that haven't yet been highlighted in other stories can make an older story feel new.

With the fire example, perhaps there are tenants who haven't yet been interviewed who could be quoted in your story, or maybe there are experts on housing law who could provide a new perspective.

TIP

The key to advancing the conversation is to just keep reporting the story until you get something new. If you weren't the first journalist to report the story, that's okay. Take the opportunity to keep digging and come up with something that feels current.

The prominence of the people involved

Big names always draw in big audiences. So, it's usually a no-brainer for newsrooms to prioritize stories that have to do with people who are prominent to their audiences. Think: celebrities, governmental officials, and other leaders.

For example, if a famous musician donates money to the school district where they grew up, that definitely makes local news in that city. But, because of that person's prominence, it will likely also make the national news.

TIP

It's easy to lean in on the prominence of the person's name and not think deeply about your story angle. But don't forget the other ways that you can and should make a story specific. For example, a story angle with a celebrity that also adds impact and timeliness is stronger than one just based on prominence.

The trendiness of the idea

Journalists want to find stories that no one is talking about, but they also want to be part of big conversations. So, when topics are trending, they want to find stories within those topics so that they can be part of it. In this case, *trending* means that people are talking about it on social media platforms and that other journalists are writing stories about it, too.

Think about when a recipe goes viral on TikTok. That recipe then spreads to other platforms such as Facebook, Instagram, and X. And then, journalists who cover lifestyle and food will also do stories about it.

But don't think this phenomenon doesn't extend to more serious stories, too. Social media trends, especially, have been responsible for bringing to light serious stories that wouldn't otherwise have gotten media attention, such as several cases of missing Black women and girls.

TIP

Some old-school journalists, especially those who view social media as frivolous, can miss out on many fresh ideas because it's where conversations happen quickly. Even if you aren't a social media user yourself, understanding how these platforms work and being comfortable navigating them can help you stay in the know.

How unusual a story is

Audiences love strange stories. As people, we love things that are odd and unusual. So, because of that, an odd detail can take a story from being boring and not very newsworthy to being extremely interesting and one that can be extremely popular with readers, viewers, or listeners. It's one of the reasons people love cute stories about animals, stories about people who are involved in strange behavior, or stories about people breaking world records.

Remember the trend of stories about people doing goat yoga? Or how engulfed people are in stories about hot dog eating contests? These are examples of very regular things that are made newsworthy by their oddness. The stories' unusual twists made them interesting.

How much conflict is present

When I was in journalism school, it used to be popular to say: "If it bleeds, it leads." That's a rather ugly way to say that gory stories about shootings and murders often land on the front pages of newspapers and are the lead stories on TV news programs.

The journalism industry has continued to evaluate its relationship with this type of coverage, thinking more about balance and ensuring less harm, but it's true that all kinds of conflict drive story coverage. But that conflict doesn't necessarily have to be violent.

Think back to elementary school when you first started to learn about how fiction stories are written. There's always some kind of conflict that drives the story. So, even when it comes to our real-life stories, there are people who don't see eye to eye, people in situations that don't align, and people who are on different sides of an issue. This is all conflict.

Examples of conflict include disagreements in organizations, union negotiations, and arguments surrounding finances. All of these subjects make for good story issues to explore.

What Drives Newsroom Decisions

Thinking about story angles is up to you as a journalist to do for yourself. Although you'll work with others in your newsroom, you have to bring ideas to the table. You can't sit back and wait for stories to be assigned to you. You have to keep the idea machine churning.

But just because you have those ideas that doesn't mean they'll get greenlit. That's even true when you have stories you absolutely love and believe in. This is because of how decisions in newsrooms are made. There is a structural hierarchy and it affects everything audiences end up seeing in their news.

Executive editors

Editors at the highest level of a journalism organization often have titles such as *executive editor, editor-in-chief,* or even *chief content officer* — the largest organizations having a mixture of many of such roles. Their greatest responsibility is to guide the overall strategy. It's why, when a place's editorial work is seen as a large success, it's deemed the executive editor's success. And, on the opposite end, when the editorial work is seen as not being up to par, it's viewed as their failure.

Here's where executive editors spend a lot of their energy to ensure the work gets done:

- **Being the face of editorial:** Editors at the top often have responsibilities that include representing the company as a brand. They're the face of the organization's editorial side, so they're often in and out of the building, traveling, attending events and conferences, and speaking on panels.
- **Hiring and making staff decisions:** It's likely no surprise, but executive and other top-level editors are only as good as the staff they have working with them. So, it's essential that they place the right people in the right roles with the right responsibilities.
- **Building and communicating strategy to midlevel editors:** Although some executive editors are more involved with the day-to-day activity of the newsroom than others, they all have meetings and events that often take them away. They simply can't be in the newsroom all the time. So, it's important for midlevel editors to know exactly what the executive editor expects, because the midlevel editors are the ones who are truly available to handle things.

Midlevel editors

Midlevel editors help the newsroom run. They may have a title such as *managing editor*, *deputy editor*, or *news director*, depending on the news organization's size and type. They're in charge of many of the daily decisions that need to be made in a newsroom. They take on more of a managerial role than executive editors, which means they make many of the tough calls surrounding coverage and what stories are produced.

It's a tough and busy job! Here are just some of the responsibilities midlevel editors usually have:

- **Setting the specific editorial goals:** Although the top-level editors may create the overall editorial strategy, midlevel editors set the goals to reach that plan.

  For example, an executive editor may give a directive to editors to increase web traffic in a specific quarter. The midlevel editors would be the ones setting goals for the number of stories, deciding the types of stories to be prioritized, and determining who will be responsible for reporting them.

- **Working as a liaison between editorial levels:** Midlevel editors are managers, helping to communicate information between executive editors and the rest of the newsroom. They also are the first to notice when there are staffing issues and needs and are the newsroom's advocates for more resources.

  For example, if a group of journalists is overworked, a managing editor would likely be responsible for trying to get a new position opened for that team to relieve the pressure on them. The managing editor would argue for money to be allotted for this new position, help get the job posted, assist in the hiring, and also manage how the responsibilities will be redistributed.

- **Monitoring metrics:** Midlevel editors generally watch metrics closely. In a newsroom, metrics are measures such as website views, time spent on the site, social media follows and clicks, and other statistics related to how people watch, listen, or read stories and other content. Midlevel editors are watching what audiences are engaging with and what they aren't.

TIP

  Metrics often drive which stories are accepted and which aren't accepted. You can use this information to your advantage! For example, if you're pitching a story that isn't normally covered, but you can show that the last time it was covered, it helped your newsroom engage with a new audience on social media, you can use that fact to persuade editors to accept this new, similar pitch.

Overall newsroom culture and interest

At the end of the day, every newsroom has its own culture, and some stories fit within that mold. Unless your newsroom has a high-level strategy to expand the image of what kinds of stories it tells, you'll probably have trouble getting a story approved that doesn't seem to follow along those lines.

Think about the personality of some of the major journalism organizations people talk a lot about in everyday discussion:

- ***Vogue:*** Fashionable, feminine, glossy
- ***The New Yorker:*** High-brow, smart, for the "coastal elite"
- **NPR:** Relatable, quirky, the people next door
- **CNN:** Straight to the point, quick, updated

Of course, this is how these organizations are perceived from the outside, but the same story would be covered at each place differently. For example, let's say you're pitching a story about a new star-studded play. Here's how you could consider pitching each one:

- ***Vogue:*** A look at how the play has a modern take on historic fashion choices
- ***The New Yorker:*** A story critiquing what the play says about society
- **NPR:** An interview with the playwright about their inspiration when writing it
- **CNN:** Updates about the who, what, when, where, why, and how about the play

Because journalists take different angles, you can see and hear similar stories that are varied enough to not be the exact same.

Working through Disagreements

Undoubtedly, there will be times in a newsroom when you want to do a story and your editor doesn't think it's a great idea. Sometimes the opposite situation — where your editor wants you to work on a story you haven't totally bought into yet — occurs. This disagreement will require some navigating because every story you work on will ultimately need your editor's approval. Luckily, there are ways to help you and your editor get on the same page.

TIP

Here are some tips to work through story ideas with your editor when you don't see eye to eye:

- **Make your case.** Is there data to support your story idea? Is there a strategic goal that may align with the need for your story? Outline why the story is a good story for the audience and also for the newsroom.
- **Ask for a compromise.** Reporters are generally working on multiple stories at once anyway. Can you balance the stories you have to do for your editors with the ones you'd like to do because you believe in them? Your editor will likely be more likely to support this plan because they'll still get the output they need from you.
- **If no is no, save it for another place.** Unfortunately, at the end of the day, if you're unable to negotiate working on your story with your editor, you can ask if you have permission to freelance it elsewhere. Depending on your employment policies, you may be allowed to work as a freelancer with permission. If not, see if you can save the idea or a version of it to pitch again at a later date.

TIP

Even if you aren't able to do a story when you first pitch it and in the way you originally wanted to do it, issues often come back around. Keep a running list of story ideas with any research or pre-reporting you've done for them, and never be afraid to rework an idea into a new story.

IN THIS CHAPTER

» Finding different types of sources

» Understanding how sources are used

» Getting the voices your story needs

Chapter 6 Finding Sources for a Story

Sources are the foundation for our reporting as journalists. Any story or a script you write is based on what you learned in your reporting, not on what you think. So, thinking through the best sources for every story is a huge part of the process.

In this chapter, I walk you through how to find the sources your story needs and build relationships with them. I also explain the different categories your sources fall into and what to expect when working with them.

What Is a Source

In journalism, a source is any person or document that gives you information to be used in reporting a story. Think of sources as ways to learn about the subject area, as well as the specific story angle you're exploring.

Journalists seek out multiple sources because they want to find out as much as they possibly can for their story, and they want to intentionally look for multiple perspectives. Looking for people who have different experiences with an issue helps you stay true to your goal of telling a full and accurate story.

In order to capture these perspectives, you have to think about all the ways information is saved and how you can then gather it. Let's say you're doing a news story about a huge vehicle pileup on a major expressway. There are many ways you might seek out information from that accident:

- **Observing the scene:** It's important for journalists to physically be at the scene of the story. There is so much information to be gathered based on what you can observe and what you can decipher with your own eyes. It's also the first step in figuring out who you should talk to, the best questions to ask, and how to gather details that others may not have.
- **Talking to those involved:** Of course, as a journalist, you always want to talk to the people who are involved in whatever you're reporting on. That isn't always possible. But in the case of this example, you'd try your best to talk to anyone involved in the pileup, if they're available.
- **Looking for eyewitnesses:** Especially because many people in the pileup may be unable to talk, eyewitnesses are key in providing multiple viewpoints of what happened. Looking for witnesses who may have been traveling in different directions, for example, could help you determine what truly happened.
- **Police reports and first-responder records:** Outside of major incidents (in which these departments will hold press conferences), their reports, which are publicly available, will serve as their perspectives on what happened.

The goal of these stories is to try to gather as much information as possible and make sense of it all. Doing so helps you re-create what happened and lay it out for your audience.

Types of Sources

Although you want to ensure that you *always* have multiple sources for every story you do, it's important to recognize that there are different types of sources that inherently bring information, different perspectives, and different purposes.

Official and unofficial

How you approach a source depends on if they're an official or unofficial source. This framing can help you think through the source's perspective and who or what they may be representing in an interview.

Official sources

Official sources are those that represent individuals and organizations or companies. These sources are chosen to speak on behalf of the brand. These are all names and titles you often see in a press release. Examples of official sources include:

- A company's chief executive officer (CEO)
- A union leader
- A police department's spokesperson
- A nonprofit organization's chief communications officer
- The White House press secretary

You always want to reach out to official sources whenever you're doing a story related to their work. But also, it's important to think about their wants and needs because it helps you think about other sources to include.

Here are some things to keep in mind about official sources:

- **They're very prepared, but guarded.** Preparation is, of course, a great thing. However, if a person is so prepared that their answers sound prewritten and unnatural, they won't be usable for your story because the audience wants to see, hear, or read quotes from sources who speak as if they're having a conversation, and they don't want canned responses.

- **Time can be limited.** Official sources are also unlikely to allow the conversation to continue to flow and may restrict you, as the interviewer, to a tight time limit. So, you'll have to prioritize certain questions and just get what you can.
- **They're motivated to get positive coverage.** At the end of the day, official sources view media as publicity for them, and they only want positive coverage. But, as journalists, it's not our job to be their publicists or marketers. You have to ask them tough but fair questions because that's your responsibility. Some people may refuse to answer these questions or choose not to speak with you when they know that this is the subject of the interview — and you should always be honest in sharing what the subject of the interview will be. Don't share the exact questions in advance, but tell the source that the interview is about one thing when it's really about something else. Be transparent in your request ahead of time.

  When journalists are doing large investigations, even then, they're honest. However, the difference may be in timing. For example, if you're doing a large investigation on a powerful government entity or company, a journalist may contact its press office last, give representatives a tight deadline to respond, and then publish. This is to ensure the integrity of the investigation.

WARNING

Regardless of the story, any time someone accuses a person or organization of anything, always reach out to them to give them an opportunity to respond. Always contact the official representative for this person or organization to ensure they're aware of the allegations. Never, ever skip this step — no matter how small the accusation may seem.

Unofficial sources

Unofficial sources may work at the same companies as official sources, but they aren't speaking on behalf of them. These sources are only speaking for themselves and are sharing their own beliefs and experiences. Examples of unofficial sources include:

- A worker at a company
- A union member
- A first responder
- A nonprofit volunteer

Unofficial sources don't have the same motivations that official sources do. It's important to think about their perspectives in stories and what you may want to talk to them about because they can and will talk more freely.

Here are some things to keep in mind about unofficial sources:

- **They don't have canned responses.** Unofficial sources don't have pre-planned, PR-approved responses. They're more likely to say what's on their mind and express to you what may be going on behind the scenes at a place they're affiliated with. There is no need to only tell you the good stuff. In fact, they're likely eager to tell you the bad stuff, too — especially when people like them are being treated poorly.
- **They truly can only represent themselves.** Because they're speaking just for themselves, everything an unofficial source says should be corroborated. Aim to talk to many unofficial sources. For example, if a worker says that managers at a company are forcing employees to break labor laws, you want to find multiple employees who will be willing to tell you the same.
- **There could be consequences for them.** There could be negative consequences for speaking to the media. As a journalist, you want to make sure that unofficial sources understand any risk they're taking by talking with you and that you aren't endangering their livelihoods without that clarity being explained.

WARNING

Many people don't really know how journalism works. As a journalist, you may assume everyone knows what you know. But your sources may not understand, for example, if their full names will be in a story, where that story will be, and so on. So, be fully transparent in explaining the process to them and making sure they understand it.

Primary and secondary sources

Where information comes from can generally be primary or secondary. Think of this as getting information firsthand versus getting it secondhand. As a journalist, you need to know and understand the differences between primary and secondary sources.

Although there is technically a category of tertiary sources, these sources aren't seen as reputable because they can be described as aggregates of primary and secondary sources.

Primary sources

Primary sources are the basis for journalism work. Think of these types of sources as first-hand accounts — people and documents that were there.

Here are some of the most common primary sources:

- People who were involved and witnesses
- Diaries, letters, and other past texts
- Speeches
- Legal and governmental documents
- Police reports and incident reports
- Original data and research

Secondary sources

Secondary sources can be helpful but in a much different way. Sometimes they analyze primary documents. Sometimes they comment or criticize them. For this reason, journalists often use these sources as part of the reporting process, but they don't often use them to gather details or facts.

In fact, some places don't use them for fact-finding at all. If someone has made an error in a secondary source, and then journalists use that secondary source for a fact instead of the original primary source, they'd be duplicating the error.

However, focusing on interpretations can add to your understanding of primary documents, so they still have their place in the reporting process. Here are some of the most common secondary sources:

- Other news articles
- Other journalists' expertise
- Analysis of research already conducted

People as Sources

Even with all the documents available, people are still your most valuable sources as a journalist. It's very rare that you'll ever do a story without talking to real people. So, it's important that you think about who to talk to as sources, where to find them, and how to make sure they're right for the story.

Finding sources

When you have a story idea that you're reporting, the first thing to do is to make a list of people you'd like to reach out to as potential sources. This list should be long and seen as just an initial brainstorm. Just add any name that could be a good interviewee, including the names of any organizations you want to find representatives from.

Here are some suggested places to look for sources:

- **Events:** Being outside and finding people in person is the most recommended way to do reporting. So, going to events is a great way to meet people who are interested in a specific topic.

  My favorite example of finding multiple types of sources in one place involves reporting a story about a farmers market in a community that is a food desert. Heading to the market on a weekend morning will put you in direct contact with:

  - Vendors who want to serve the community
  - Shoppers who are happy to have access to fresh produce

- The organizers who want to provide the market in this particular area

  Just one place would give a journalist doing this story access to many sources with three different perspectives.

- **Websites:** Use the websites of organizations, companies, and places to scan for people who may be good sources for stories. Even when reaching out to an organization's media department, requesting to interview a specific person and providing an actual name is always better than requesting a general representative.

  For example, for a story about science, a science museum's website will show which curators are experts in which areas. Inquiring about a specific curator will ensure you won't waste their time or yours.

- **Social media:** Social media is a place where people look to meet people and communicate. So, as the online world continues to expand, more ways to find sources pop up:
  - Conducting general searches on platforms such as X (formerly known as Twitter) can help find people to reach out to based on what they express online.
  - Scanning forums such as Reddit can help create leads.
  - Joining online communities such as Facebook Groups can be a targeted way to find people.

Vetting sources

After you find people that you want to reach out to, it's essential to vet them. It's not enough to be wowed by a professional-looking website, for example, or a nice profile photo. You want to ensure that:

- **People are who they say they are.** Some people are just not who they claim to be. You'll need to do a little digging and at least look and see if everything makes sense.
- **You know about any relevant ties people have.** If a person's connections are likely influencing their perspective, you have to disclose that in your story or not use

them. For example, if you're doing a story about what everyday citizens think of the president and a potential source is a political strategist who was a consultant on the president's campaign, they're no longer a good source for this story.

- **People don't have an obvious history of being untruthful.** Some people may be known for lying or may have been untruthful when interviewed in the past. These types of instances are ones you want to look for and avoid.

Investigative journalists have tools that help them do deeper background checks on people. That's not something you realistically could or would do for every story. You can lean mostly on a Google search and a scan of a person's social media accounts to do the level of vetting you require.

When vetting people, think generally about the five Ws (with the relevancy of each of these dependent on the story and their place in that story):

- **Who:** Does their LinkedIn say they are who they say they are? Is that their true career?
- **What:** Has this person talked about the topic they'll be talking to you about?
- **Where:** Is someone claiming to be in one place but all of their posts are geotagged in another?
- **When:** Is it possible that they could have been a witness to something based on their posts?
- **Why:** Would they receive any other benefits from talking to you besides sharing the truth of what happened or what they know?

Developing long-term sources

You put so much effort into finding people to interview that you shouldn't look at them as just sources for a singular story, but as people you're building long-term working relationships with.

Here are some reasons to think of your sources in this way:

- **Investing time:** It takes a great deal of time to find sources in the first place. If for every story you have to start all over again, it can take a long time.
- **Deeper stories:** It takes time to gain trust with people, which is especially important when reporting stories that are on more sensitive topics. Every time you interview sources, you show them you're trustworthy and can handle tougher stories.
- **Being first in line:** Journalists who take the time to build these types of relationships also get some of the best stories because they become sources' first call when news happens.

The best advice I ever received was to not always wait until I need something from a source to reach out to them. Part of being a good journalist is building relationships. Go and meet people in places and at organizations you think you may be interested in reporting on later and introduce yourself. Learn what's going on. Observe the area. Ask questions. Get on their email lists.

This type of work is extra important if you'll be reporting in a neighborhood or community you aren't familiar with. It shows that you care about investing time into this relationship and that you aren't trying to be extractive: coming into the neighborhood, taking what you need for a story, and leaving and never coming back.

The Voices Your Story Needs

When doing a story that's about a social issue or problem, thinking through your sources becomes extra significant. That's because, in these instances, you're making really big editorial judgments about what voices you're amplifying and including.

Here are some ways to think about how to approach a story about an issue in a fuller way and some specific voices to seek out:

» **Someone affected by it:** People are experts in their own experiences. So, you'd never want to do a story about an issue without including the perspective of at least one person who is experiencing it. For example, you couldn't complete a story about a city's growing unhoused population without including someone who is currently unhoused.

» **Someone who studies it:** Researchers and scholars who can serve as more independent expert voices can help legitimize what people are saying they're experiencing.

» **Someone making decisions about it:** Social issues are shaped by policy, so speaking with those who make such policies and laws would bring in a separate perspective and allow you to ask tough questions.

» **Someone trying to change it:** Advocates, changemakers, activists, and more provide different viewpoints about what needs to be done to fix or end social issues — viewpoints that you want to include.

Always remember that voices that are often the least prioritized are those who are most affected by a social issue. So, whenever possible, you want to try to balance out that disparity.

What to include when reaching out

When it's time to actually reach out to potential sources, there is some essential information that sources need to know in order to make a decision on whether they want to talk to a journalist. Your goal should be to give them as much information as possible in order for them to make that decision while not trying to overwhelm them.

When writing your script for your phone call or drafting your email, here are some items to prioritize:

» **Your journalistic affiliation:** What media outlet is this particular story for?

» **What the overall story is about:** What's the story topic that you're working on?

» **What you specifically want to interview this source about:** Don't send sources interview questions beforehand, but you can tell them the focus of the interview. How does this fit within the greater, overall story you're working on?

» **Any details about timing, place, or mode of interview:** Will it be in-person, on Zoom, or by phone? When do you have to conduct it by?

TIP

Don't be afraid to pick up the phone and call people. Although the rise in hybrid and virtual workplaces has made work habits less predictable, most places still have some kind of phone line or have phone numbers routed to employees' cell phones. And when you aren't sure who exactly to email, phone is usually the quickest and easiest way to reach the right department. For example, if you're trying to reach a museum's media department, pick up the phone, and if needed, leave a voicemail.

On or off the record? What it means

As you're getting your sources, keep in mind that there will sometimes be stories in which you'll need to negotiate with your sources — and with your editor. When the information a source tells you is extremely sensitive, what you use and how you use it can be tackled in multiple ways.

You've heard the term *off the record* to denote something that can't be used at all. But there are ways to protect a source's identity and need for secrecy while being as specific as possible to your audience.

Here is the spectrum of ways that anonymity can look:

» **Off the record:** This means that sources do not expect this information to be used in any way that could be attributed to them. As a journalist, you can use the information solely as a tip, but you need to find another source in order to report on it.

Reporters who cover crime and policing have off-the-record conversations with police officers quite often because they commonly have information that would be unsafe if tracked back to them. In those cases, the journalists have to find other evidence or sources to protect the original source's anonymity.

- **On deep background:** This means that sources are aware that the information will likely be used, but they know that it may be used just for more reporting. It's usually not enough information to report right out because it can't be attributed to anyone.

  Examples of information that are on deep background may be learning how a private system works or learning about an unfair practice.

- **On background:** Sometimes, journalists report out information that is on background by attributing it to a general group of people or possibly by being a little bit more specific by sharing a type of position or a job level. The key is to make sure that the descriptor is still general enough that audiences can't guess or assume who was a source.

  For example, in a story about assault on a college football team, reporters spoke with multiple former players and because that could be hundreds of men within the time period specified, they could use descriptors like "former football players" or "players on the offensive team" instead of identifying any specific player names.

- **On the record:** Explain to sources everything that will be used in a story, which — in addition to their full name — could also be things such as age, occupation and title, neighborhood, and more. This varies by story and by journalism outlet, so it's important to be clear.

REMEMBER

These definitions are widely used, but different people have different ideas of where these lines are drawn. For example, some people don't make a differentiation between something being on background and it being on deep background. So it's important to discuss what you mean in detail with your sources so you're on the same page.

IN THIS CHAPTER

» Navigating the interview process

» Communicating with your interviewees

» Quoting your interviewees in your final story

Chapter 7
Conducting Interviews

After you've gotten people to agree to an interview, it may seem like the hardest part is over. For many new journalists, that's often the case. But the truth is that the interview is where your skills can really shine. It's the part of the process where you can also lean into your natural curiosity, listening skills, and ability to ask questions. Being able to navigate conversations may be why you wanted to be a journalist in the first place.

However, even the most skilled interviewers spend a ton of time preparing before speaking with a source and working through what was discussed after it's over. Although this process can be slightly different depending on who you're interviewing and what your subject or story angle will be, there are some steps that are generally accepted practices in journalism interviewing.

In this chapter, I explain the interview process and how you can best prepare and work with sources before, during, and after an interview. I also give tips on taking care with vulnerable sources.

The Interview Process

The interview process itself involves much more than simply the time you spend asking questions. It starts long before the actual interview begins and, in a way, continues until your story is completed. This approach is different from getting information from other sources such as documents.

Because interviews involve people, your goal should be to think about this process as a relationship. The thoughts, concerns, and feelings of your interviewees are important. As a journalist, you're requesting information to support your work. Sometimes there is little benefit for the interviewees to share their stories, so you can't treat these interactions as simple transactions. They can be complicated and deserve a high level of care.

TIP

Approaching the interview process as a significant information-finding mission will help you get what you need for your story while also helping you gain insight into an interviewee's unique perspective on an issue or topic.

Doing your research

The first step in preparing for an interview is researching the topic you'll be talking about with your source. This step is essential in multiple ways:

- **It establishes you as an expert.** When interviewers come to an interview seemingly uninformed about a topic, they appear to be novices. Doing your research beforehand can help you set the tone in the interview that you're an experienced interviewer.
- **It shows that you're respectful of your interviewee's time.** Your interviewee has the taken time to speak with you. They likely don't want to feel as if they're wasting their time explaining ideas to you that you could've researched beforehand.
- **It helps you better understand your interviewee's responses.** The better you know the subject you'll be speaking about, the better you'll understand the answers they give you. This will also help you ask better follow-up questions to those responses.

But when you're ready to start your research, where do you start? Here are some tips on doing a thorough job.

1. **Do a general search on the topic.**

   Starting with a more general search can be helpful in gaining important background on a wide topic before diving into the specific focus you'll be reporting on. For example, if you're looking to do a story on how increased air pollution is making people sick in a certain place, you may want to first look into the science behind air pollution in general.

2. **Read, watch, and listen to what other journalists have done.**

   Good journalism often builds on other good journalism. This means that some of the best and most influential stories happen because a group of journalists have diligently covered the topic before. It's highly likely that the story you want to cover has been covered in some way before — and that's okay! But you should know what previous stories have found.

3. **Do a deep dive into your interviewee.**

   If you're interviewing someone who is interviewed a lot, or someone who may publish their own work, you probably have a lot to learn about what they've already shared. This information can be key in asking smart questions later.

Even if your interviewee has said or written something before, if you'd like to use it in *your* story, it's always best to bring it back up in an interview. But here's where phrasing is essential: You want to let the person know that you did do your work before the interview and that you're simply following up on what you've learned by researching them. Instead of simply asking the question, explain where you learned it from and that you'd like them to expand on it or draw from it and why.

Here's an example of asking an artist to expand on something they've said before:

> I read in the *Tribune* how your inspiration for this exhibit was your family's story. Can you expand on how that shows up in this work? It seems to be very influential in the pieces we're talking about.

Preparing questions

After doing your research, it's time to start drafting questions for your interview. These questions are to keep you on task during to make sure you ask all the essential questions you need to ask for your story.

Easing into the interview

Your initial questions can help you build rapport with your interviewee. Ask relevant questions, but ones that your interviewees may be most excited to talk about.

For example, starting off with questions about the excitement surrounding a new project will feel like a more natural beginning than questions about the project's challenges and problems. Those can come later, and it will feel like a natural transition when you dive into the tougher part of the interview.

An exception to this is if you're interviewing a busy political figure or another person you can only interview for a short amount of time. In these cases, you'll want to hop directly into your most important questions. These people are generally comfortable speaking with journalists because they're interviewed so often.

Adding facts and details to your question notes

You won't be reading your questions verbatim so it's helpful to add any details that will help you sound more knowledgeable about what you'll be asking.

Your notes can hold quotes, references to key dates or names, or any other facts that would be helpful to remember if your interviewee doesn't mention them but you need to remember yourself in order to keep the conversation going.

Writing more questions than you think you'll need

Some interviewees have short answers to questions, while others have answers so long that they answer questions you haven't even asked yet. So, it's really hard to guess ahead of time how many questions you may need for certain interviews.

For example, if you're writing a profile that's all about a person, you'll want to have a long enough interview with enough responses to write that story. Fifteen minutes just wouldn't do!

But also, just because you write more questions, it doesn't mean you have to ask them all. There should still be a priority. Know which low-priority questions you'll likely skip because they're less important. These questions are technically just your backup options.

Preparing questions in advance should serve as a guide and not a script though. You should listen to your interviewees' answers in order to ask natural follow-ups. You should also jump around your question list and change the order of when and how you ask your planned questions based on the person's responses.

Interviews are conversations. Although it can be easy to forget, don't let the transactional nature of what you need to get out of the interview take precedence over the conversation. Be sure to:

- Really listen to your interviewee's answers.
- Be open to the conversation going a slightly different way sometimes.
- Not try to force people to answer how you'd like them to answer.

Taking care with vulnerable sources

You'll interview some people who you'll need to treat with extra care. This is because they may or may not know the effects of speaking with you. Those who may fall into this category include:

- **People at risk of experiencing violence:** Those talking to you about dangerous activity could be at risk of experiencing violence themselves. For example, a survivor of an attack speaking out about their attacker or a bystander of a crime could put themselves in danger by doing an interview with you.

- **People at risk of being arrested or harassed by authorities:** Those who may be admitting fault of any kind or could be assuming legal liability for something may need extra protection in a story. This is common in cities and regions with large immigrant populations, for example, in which there may or may not be people who are undocumented. A story about how a local company is abusing immigrant labor, for example, may put an unwanted spotlight on community members.
- **People at risk of losing benefits:** The only way to hold people in power accountable is to speak with people who are affected by unfair policies and practices. However, that could put those people at risk of losing needed benefits — for example, affordable housing vouchers, Supplemental Nutrition Assistance Program (SNAP) benefits, or medical assistance.
- **People whose families or loved ones may be at risk:** The risk doesn't stop at the interviewees themselves. It can also extend to their family and others. So, it's important for you, as the journalist, to think through what information could be harmful and if they may be sharing details that could also affect another person.
- **People who have experienced significant tragedy:** People may not know in advance how your questions may affect them. An interview can trigger feelings from traumatic experiences, even if they happened years ago.

Look through other similar stories for ideas on how other journalists have handled the protection of their sources in the past.

These are undoubtedly complicated situations. But there are some simple ways to help you add in extra care:

- **Talk them through the interview process.** For many vulnerable sources, you may be their first interviewer ever. Explain the full process to them, especially how stories are edited and published, and include any specific steps you or your news organization may take. Then get their *informed consent,* or clear permission, to speak with them.

For example, if your organization always uses a separate person to call them and check the facts of the story, let them know in advance. If a person they don't know calls and asks them about the details they've shared with you — the person they built a relationship with — they may be unpleasantly surprised. Explain that using an extra person as a fact-checker can help you to get it right — and it's an extra layer of protection for them, too.

» **Add in extra time.** Interviews may go longer because of these extra steps. Also, your interviewee may need extra processing time during certain questions or they may want to go back to something you've already covered. They may take the conversation in a completely different direction for a moment while they try to answer. Don't rush the process and make sure you don't have anywhere to run off to immediately after that would push you to do so.

» **Talk with an editor or a trusted colleague.** These types of interviews are much harder to navigate. As a journalist, you want to do a thorough job. But you also don't want to forget that you shouldn't create additional harm. Finding this balance can be complicated, especially for newer journalists.

If you're working in a traditional newsroom, your editor is there to help. You don't need to wait until there are issues in your reporting to go to them for assistance. Consult with your editor during the interview prep and planning stage on some ways to handle your source.

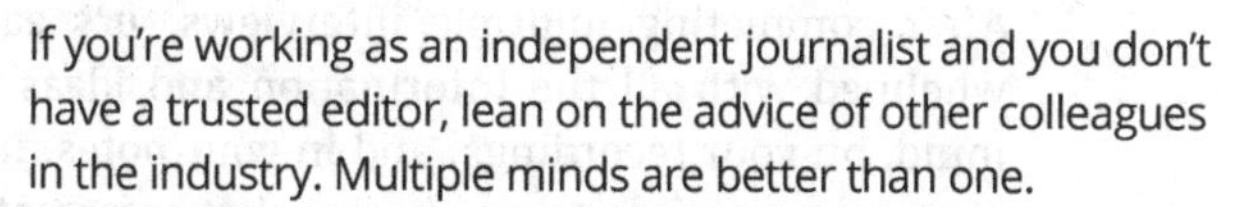

If you're working as an independent journalist and you don't have a trusted editor, lean on the advice of other colleagues in the industry. Multiple minds are better than one.

» **Stay up-to-date on trauma-informed reporting techniques.** *Trauma-informed reporting* is a set of practices that prevents journalists from retraumatizing the people they interview. It's a new term and an even newer field of study that will continue to grow, but it involves certain practices such as:

- Understanding trauma and how it affects the brain
- Overexplaining ideas, the process, and impact
- Respecting interviewees' boundaries when they say "no"
- Thinking about your own mental health

REMEMBER

Your job is to think of the multiple risks that could happen from your reporting because, as a journalist, your job is not to create any additional harm for your sources. This is especially true when they may not know or realize that risk exists. After ensuring your interviewee understands the risk, you and your editor can talk through any extra protections you may want to take in these cases. For example, you may want to just use the first names of the undocumented workers you interview or you may want to make sure the faces of an interviewee's family are hidden.

After the Interview

After you've completed your interviews, the real work begins. It's essential to think through what happens after you've spoken with people because you then become the conduit for what they've told you. This is a huge responsibility. When you get it wrong, you're sharing a misinterpreted version of them. But when you get it right, you're able to properly express their viewpoints.

Synthesizing interview discussions

After completing multiple interviews, it's easy to feel overwhelmed with all the information and ideas that are in your mind, on your recordings, and in your notes. It's a lot. But here are some practices to synthesize that information and help get you on the right track:

- **Logging tape:** Before the popularity of transcription services powered by artificial intelligence (AI), logging tape was a common practice — primarily for journalists working in audio and video. It involves going through your interview tape and marking what topics are discussed and their corresponding time codes so you can easily find the info later.

Logging tape creates a detailed summary of every interview, and even if you're using a transcription service, it can be a helpful way to document what you heard because it forces you to listen to the recordings before you forget what you discussed. Today, you can do this in many ways — most transcription services allow you to add notes and highlight the transcripts they generate.

» **Sketching:** Stories of all mediums have a structure, and after completing your interviews, it's essential to think through yours. Imagine your story as something you're building with blocks. Based on what you now know:

  - Which blocks fit where?
  - Where do your interviewees' viewpoints fit in this structure?
  - Are there any remaining holes in your story as far as interviewees and perspectives are concerned?

» **Outlining:** Outlining may feel unnecessary, but it definitely is the key to synthesizing what you've learned and transferring it into a story draft. Regardless of the mode — written, audio, or video — you should have an outline before you actually write your stories. Your outline is your guide, and it can grow from your sketch and your interview logs.

TIP

I like to take my outline and then add in what I think is my best interviewee quotes. For some stories, such as stories that are very feature-based with lots of needed voices, this helps me get close to a filled-in draft. From there, I go back to the top of the story and write through it — modifying and deleting quotes as necessary. This isn't the only way to go from outline to draft, but it helped me tremendously when I was starting out, especially with longer stories that intimidated me.

Choosing quotes

When you have hours of interview tape and pages of transcripts, how do you decide what to use? Some interviewees are so compelling that you may want to use almost everything. But that's not possible. It's your job to pull out the best of the best.

TIP

When you choose quotes, look for:

- **Quotes with emotion:** You can explain facts yourself. And generally, because you know how to be concise in your writing, you can generally reshare that kind of information more succinctly than your interviewees spoke it. So, what you want to focus on is finding quotes that share emotion — whether it's anger, sadness, joy, or anything else.
- **Quotes with specific, strong language:** Many times interviewees use language that you want to be attributed to them without paraphrasing it. For example, if a source calls a decision "catastrophic," using their exact wording is stronger than just explaining that the decision could have adverse effects. It also better and more accurately describes what the source meant and their perspective.
- **Quotes that translate well in your medium:** Audiences take in information differently depending on how they're consuming information, and you can adjust for that with quotes. For example, in print, quotes need to be short and tight and not too long; otherwise, they won't be easily understood. But in video and audio, that same long quote may be powerful and useful because you can hear the person as they're saying it. For example, quotes with long pauses may show certain kinds of emotions. But those pauses won't translate to print.

Following up

After an interview is over, some reporters think the job is done. But when you think of your sources as people you want to have continued relationships with, you'll see why it's important to follow up with them afterward.

After completing interviews, here are some things to keep in mind:

- **Fact-checking:** Will you or anyone else need to follow up with your interviewee to fact-check what's in the story? Fact-checking practices vary, and some places still do the more traditional way of fact-checking by having someone call up sources and ask them to confirm every fact. If this happens, you should let your source know that they may be contacted by a fact-checker later.

» **Photography:** Will a photographer or editor be contacting the source to schedule a photo shoot? Similar to fact-checking, you can prevent any confusion by explaining this to your source in advance.

» **Publishing date and place:** When will the story be published? If you know the date, be sure to share that information with your source. If not, share any links and relevant information (for example, future re-air dates and times) in an email, phone call, or text message.

REMEMBER

Most of the people you interview as sources won't really know the ins and outs of the journalism process. And even if they do, every journalism outlet has its own preferred practices and processes.

How to Quote Interviewees

You may think that there's just one way to quote the people you interview as sources, but there are actually many. It's helpful to understand the different types of quotes there are and when to employ them.

Paraphrase

Most of what you've taken in and synthesized will be turned into *paraphrasing* — using your own words to describe what the interviewee said. This goes back to the idea that much of what you're told is best explained concisely.

Here are some things to keep in mind when paraphrasing:

» **When it's best:** Paraphrasing is best when you're writing about facts and other kinds of information.

» **When it may not work:** When specificity can help the audience better understand what the source said, you may lose some details when paraphrasing.

» **Rules for using it:** Pay attention to attribution placement and verb tense.

- In print stories, attribution is often at the end of a paraphrased sentence and in past tense (for example, "An electrical issue in the building caused the massive fire, authorities said").
- In broadcast stories, attribution goes at the beginning and is in present tense (for example, "Authorities say an electrical issue in the building caused the massive fire").

Use quotes when the interviewee is showing emotion in what they're discussing. Otherwise, paraphrase.

Direct quote

A *direct quote* is the exact words a source has spoken.

Here are some important things to know about using direct quotes:

» **When they're best:** Direct quotes are best to show emotion and interviewees' explicit feelings.

» **When they may not work:** If a source's sentences are not clear enough to understand without significant modification, direct quotes may not work.

» **Rules for using them:** The tense and placement in direct quotes are similar to that of paraphrased quotes. But for written direct quotes, there are several rules most newspaper and print media use:

- Ellipses (. . .) take the place of cut words if a place allows modifying quotes.
- When you have to clarify wording by rewriting it, brackets ([ ]) are used to indicate what you modified.

- Most places prefer that the noun in attribution goes before the verb — "John Doe said" instead of "said John Doe," for example.

Partial quote

A *partial quote* is a mix between a direct quote and a paraphrased one. It involves using just a word or phrase in quotation marks within a paraphrased sentence or other written sentence in a piece.

Here are some ways to view partial quotes:

» **When they're best:** When you only need to use part of a source's exact words, a partial quote works great. It also helps if some or all of the remaining quote is not easily understood and would need to be significantly edited, which you don't do ethically.

» **When they may not work:** Partial quotes usually work for most instances, but they may not be a substitute when a full quote is best.

» **Rules for using them:** The tense and placement are similar to that of paraphrased and direct quotes because they're just part of the sentence.

Dialogue

Similar to what you would see in a book, *dialogue* involves capturing a conversation by using the direct quotes of multiple people. Dialogue isn't used that often in most journalistic stories.

There aren't many specific rules regarding dialogue, but it can appear differently depending on the medium. Sometimes it's used to help the audience read, hear, or view a scene. It can also be used to share something that's difficult to explain without such a reenactment.

AMPLIFYING THE PERSPECTIVES OF MARGINALIZED PEOPLE

Historically, marginalized people haven't been prioritized in journalism. People have been — and sometimes, continue to be — excluded due to their race, ethnicity, gender identity, sexual orientation, ability, socioeconomic status, and other factors. So, as a journalist, it's your ethical responsibility to not only identify these groups but also ask yourself a series of important questions:

- Who is marginalized in this story?
- Who has not been empowered to speak up?
- Who has been intentionally silenced?

You can incorporate newer journalism practices into your daily work to help amplify these perspectives:

- **Engagement journalism** allows community participation in the reporting process.
- **Solidarity journalism** centers marginalized groups in the framing of issues.
- **Solutions journalism** focuses on responses to problems rather than the problems themselves.
- **Trauma-informed journalism** teaches how to prevent retraumatizing sources during reporting.

Looking for resources on these practices can help you ensure that everyone's voice is heard as you do a better job of listening.

IN THIS CHAPTER

» **Understanding the role math plays in journalism**

» **Getting good data for your stories**

» **Memorizing common computations**

Chapter 8 Doing Your Math

Many journalists joke that they didn't get into this industry to deal with numbers. That's because there's a misconception that as long as you're great at words, you're a great reporter.

But that ideology is simply not true. It's a reason why studying journalism isn't just about writing (the way it is when you study English or creative writing, for example). Journalism is also about finding stories, adding contexts to them, and explaining to your audience why they're important. To do that, you need good data.

Here are some roles that data can play in a journalism story:

- **Data can help formulate the question on which a story is based.** For example, why are drivers in poorer neighborhoods exponentially ticketed more than drivers in more affluent neighborhoods in the same city?
- **Data can add context to an issue being discussed.** For example, two years after the rollout of the mental health crisis hotline, 988, a majority of Americans say they aren't familiar with it.

- **Data can support a theory.** For example, climate change is causing higher temperatures in areas across the United States.
- **Data can dispel myths or give weight to one side of an argument.** For example, analysts estimate a significant dip in back-to-school sales this August, but data shows that shoppers are more likely to take advantage of deals this year than in recent years.

Think of numbers as a way to have the strongest story possible. Focus on pulling in statistics and data that make the most sense for the story you're telling. It doesn't have to be complicated.

Getting Good Data

To start, it's important to get good data that you can trust. But where do you find it? Here are some common places to get data for journalism stories:

- **U.S. Census:** Census numbers tell a lot about what's going on in the country, and the U.S. Census is one of the most reliable sources of data. Not only can you get information about population demographics such as age, ethnicity, and household size, but you can also get a wealth of information about the economics of a particular area.

  The U.S. Census Bureau website (`www.census.gov`) continues to improve. You can easily create a table of specific information you need, and the data is so detailed, it can be drilled down to an individual zip code or a group of blocks within a census tract — small divisions of a county.

  You can find out how to better use U.S. Census tools through its learning hub called Census Academy (`www.census.gov/data/academy.html`). These courses are free, with videos guiding you through each module. You can even request an in-person or online training for your newsroom for free if you need a specialized training.

- **Governmental websites:** Websites for cities, counties, states, and the federal government often report certain information on a monthly, quarterly, or annual basis.

Here are some types of information to search for in your municipality's data portal:

- Employee salaries, including for elected officials
- Education information, such as budgets and facilities information
- Parks and recreation data, such as beach water quality and library visitor information
- Public safety data around crime, policing, and arrests
- Transportation information, such as traffic crashes, public transportation ridership, and parking information
- Service requests about issues such as potholes, tree debris, and street light outages

» **Freedom of Information Act (FOAI) requests:** There is some public information that you, as a journalist and just as a regular person, have the right to request if it isn't easily available in a database or data portal. If there is a specific data request you have, you can submit a FOIA request.

Submitting a FOIA request looks differently for every governmental agency. To look up the process for the agency you're reaching out to, search the web (or the agency's website) for "FOIA" or "public information officer."

In your FOIA request, you'll want to be as specific as possible about what you're requesting and in what form. For example, if you want the info to be in a spreadsheet, explain that in the request. This is extremely important because FOIA officers can deny requests that are "unduly burdensome." It's a good idea to try your best to use the words and categories they use to make that clear.

Logs of previous FOIA requests may be an available dataset that's easy to download from a data portal. If so, viewing those logs can help you determine if your request may have already been filled recently. And if not, it can help you properly formulate the request so you know what categories are available. For example, if you're requesting data on recent traffic accidents, you may not know how locations are listed. Are they listed by nearest address, coordinates, or street intersections? Viewing previous info could help.

» **Polls and surveys:** Asking people their opinions on, their awareness of, or their plans to do something is one of the best ways to get an understanding of how the general public — or a subset of it — thinks about a topic. You can conduct polls by making phone calls, sending emails, or asking people questions on the street. The goal is to talk to a sample of people who represent the greater group that you're trying to understand.

If you work at a large newsroom, there will likely be teams of people whose job it is to conduct such polls. For example, places such as *The New York Times* conduct their own polls during election season. Similarly, you can do polls yourself in your newsroom, or you can team up with non-bias researchers such as those at universities to conduct them properly if you don't feel you have the resources.

People are probably most familiar with political polls because this type of surveying is often discussed over and over during election cycles. And in this case, it's often done in two ways:

- **Polling the same people over a period of time:** This approach is much harder, but it can be helpful in analyzing people's attitudes over time based on changes. For example, some major media organizations polled the same people for both the 2020 and 2024 presidential elections on who they planned to vote for and what topics they cared most about in making their decisions. This is difficult to do, and these polls often have fewer participants because it's time-consuming and requires buy-in from those who are polled.
- **Speaking with new, randomly selected people each time:** When using random samples, you need to choose a large number of people and ensure that those selected represent certain backgrounds, such as race and ethnicity, age, and socioeconomic status. For example, if you're doing a survey about U.S. job salaries after graduation, it's important to have enough people who represent people of varying backgrounds in order to see if there are any trends related not only to majors or programs, but also to geographic differences in the cost of living.

» **Organizations/companies:** Although not all organizations and companies share their data, many do. This practice can vary greatly based on the industry and type of organization. Nonprofit organizations, for example, are required to disclose certain information, such as how they spend their money, so they often have data easily available because it's public knowledge.

  Varying levels of information may be shared based on such requirements, though. For example, all universities must share certain data with the U.S. Department of Education. This helps ensure that institutions aren't taking advantage of students and employees. But public universities get much of their funding from state sources and will likely have to share additional information that a private university may not have to disclose.

  Of course, you can always request information that you can't find on an organization's website. They may not share it, if it's something they aren't required to disclose, but it doesn't hurt to request it.

TIP

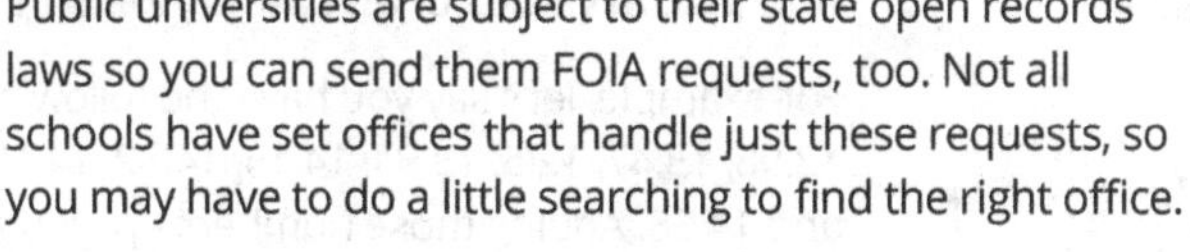
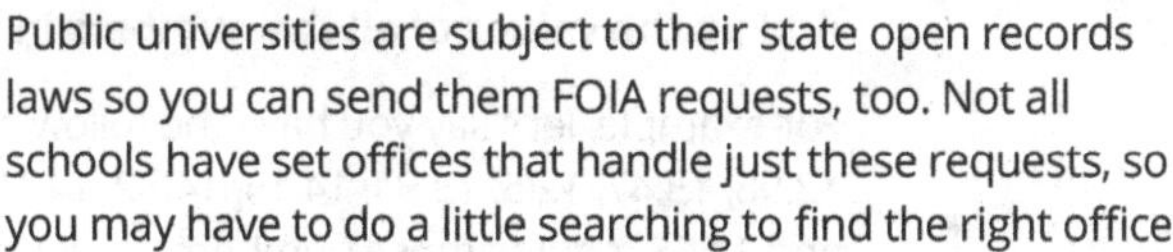

Public universities are subject to their state open records laws so you can send them FOIA requests, too. Not all schools have set offices that handle just these requests, so you may have to do a little searching to find the right office.

After you have your data, it's essential that you do the right calculations for it to be helpful. Data journalism, itself, is a specialized skill. But all journalists should have some basic knowledge of how to correctly and accurately compute certain common calculations that come up often in the everyday story (read on for more on this subject).

Finding the Average

Quite often, journalistic stories talk about the average person — the average person doing a certain thing or in a certain situation or dealing with a certain problem. But in order to do that, you have to understand what the actual average is. There are two calculations to represent this: the mean and the median. And there are certain situations in which one or the other is the best to use.

Mean

The term *mean* is often used interchangeably with *average* because it simply means that it's the average of all numbers in a dataset. The weight of all the numbers is equal.

Examples of using a mean could be:

- » The average Social Security check seniors receive
- » The average hourly wages
- » The average cost of tuition

Using the average for these examples gives a fair representation of the groups they represent because there aren't likely enough outliers who would fall extremely above or below this average range.

Calculating the mean is extremely simple:

1. **Add up the values of all the numbers in the dataset.**

   For example, let's say you have the following numbers: 12.98, 13.47, 12.5, 13.94, 14.13, 14.32, 14.15, 10.95, 10.74, and 14.58. Adding those numbers up, you get 131.76.

2. **Divide that sum by how many numbers there are.**

   Your dataset includes ten numbers total, so dividing 131.76 by 10, you get a mean of 13.176, or 13.18 if you're rounding to the nearest hundredth.

REMEMBER

The goal of using the mean is to be fair and accurate — and that's your ethical responsibility as a journalist. The numbers you share should align with this goal.

Median

Many times the mean is not the best way to represent an average, even if it's technically the way to calculate it. In these cases, there are numbers in a dataset that are, outliers so calculating the mean would show a skewed average.

That's why we have the *median* (the middle value in a set of values). When you use the media, you can create a better and more accurate estimate of what number is truly average when some numbers are much lower than most in a dataset and/or some are much higher. Because of this, the median is often used in news stories that deal with money and cost, but it's helpful in many other types of stories, too.

Here are some examples of when you may want to use the median:

- The median costs of homes in an area
- The median salary in an industry
- The median age of workers

Calculating the median is not as simple as calculating the mean, but it's very doable after you do some initial organizing:

1. **Organize the numbers in the dataset in order of value.**

   For example, let's say you have the following numbers: $52,300; $54,800; $29,800; $53,700; $92,300; $51,600; $78,500; $55,900; $38,400; and $56,200.

2. **Arrange the numbers in order from lowest to highest.**

   In this example, that would be as follows: $29,800; $38,400; $51,600; $52,300; $53,700; $54,800; $55,900; $56,200; $78,500; and $92,300.

3. **Find the middle number.**

   If there is an odd amount of numbers, the number in the middle is the median. If there is an even amount of numbers, find the two numbers in the middle, and then find the mean of those two numbers.

   In the example, we have ten numbers, so the two middle numbers would be the fifth and the sixth — or $53,700 and $54,800. Now add those two numbers ($53,700 + $54,800 = $108,500) and divide by 2 to get the median ($108,500 ÷ 2 = $54,250).

TIP

If you have many numbers in your dataset, it's easier to calculate the median by using the Median function in a spreadsheet app such as Microsoft Excel or Google Sheets.

Remember that the median differs from the mean because it takes into account outliers. If you're struggling to see which measure you should use, look to see if experts in the industry use mean or median. You can always calculate both to see the difference in how much the outliers in a dataset change an average. In the median example I walk you through in this section, the average of those ten salaries was $56,350, whereas the mean was $54,250. Depending on your story, that may or may not be a significant difference.

Calculating Change

Many journalism stories are built on monitoring change — an increase, a decrease, or something staying the same. Think about crime stories or evaluating solutions to major problems. In these types of stories, analyzing change (or the lack thereof) is the basis for reporting.

Percent change

One of the easiest and most common ways to express change is by sharing a percent change. This is helpful because it compares data for the same thing over a period of time.

Examples of using a percentage could be:

- The decrease in home sales from this time last year
- The decrease in crime over the past six months
- The increase in electricity use in the summer months

Calculating the percentage is simple:

1. **Subtract the old value from the new value.**

   For example, let's say there were two murders in Springfield in 2023 and five murders in Springfield in 2024. If you're trying to show the percent change between 2023 and 2024, you would subtract the old value (the one from 2023) from the new value (the one from 2024), like this: 5 – 2 = 3.

2. **Divide that number by the old value.**

   In this example, divide 3 by 2, and you get 1.5.

3. **Multiply by 100 to get the percent.**

   Multiply 1.5 by 100, and you get 150 percent. There was a 150 percent increase in the murder rate from 2023 to 2024 in Springfield.

TIP

Some people forget whether to subtract the old value from the new one or the new one from the old. It's an extremely common mistake. To remember, memorize *NOO*, which stands for:

(NEW – OLD) ÷ OLD

Percentage point change

Percentage point change can sometimes be confused with simple percent change. But there is one key difference: Percentage points represent the difference between percentages and not between the values themselves.

Common examples of using a percentage point change could be:

- The increase in inflation
- The decrease in the corporate tax rate
- The increase in poll percentage points

To calculate the change in percentage points, subtract the old percentage from the new percentage. The resulting percentage is the change in percentage points.

This calculation is simple, but it's important to know when and why to use it. Think of what a percentage is: When you calculate the *percent change* of something, you're essentially showing how it changed proportional to its old or original amount. (***Remember:*** New minus the old, all divided by the old.) When you're comparing *percentage points,* you aren't looking at that original amount — you're just looking at how that percentage changed.

Let's work on an example. According to the U.S. Census Bureau, in 2011, 87.6 percent of adults aged 25 and older had high school degrees. In 2021, this percentage increased to 91.1 percent. To find the change in percentage point, subtract the old percentage from the new percentage: 91.1 – 87.6 = 3.5. So, the percentage of adults aged 25 who graduated from high school increased by 3.5 percentage points.

You use percentage points because you're comparing the change in two percentages, *not* the change in the original values.

You would *not* say that the graduate rate increased 3.5 percent — that's not accurate. To calculate the *percent change*, you need the actual values. In 2011, it was 176,504,000. In 2021, it was 204,526,000 people. The percent change would be 15.87 percent, or 16 percent if you round up.

REMEMBER

When you think more deeply about why you use certain calculations, it will help you choose the right one.

IN THIS CHAPTER

» Thinking through the ethics of accuracy

» Executing the fact-checking process

» Controlling and minimizing errors

Chapter 9 Fact-Checking a Story

Fact-checking is an essential part of reporting but one that is not always treated with the significance it deserves. It's often taught as the last thing to do before you publish — something small and insignificant.

But fact-checking should be considered throughout the reporting process. And when it's not, there can be serious consequences, not just for journalists and media organizations but also for the people, places, and things we report on.

Think about breaking news today. When a celebrity dies, many people rush to be first to report the news out — forgetting just how often facts in these stories can be wrong, including whether the person has actually died.

Incorrectly reporting such an event causes harm to the celebrity's family and friends and also causes you and your organization to lose credibility. Your audience has to trust that the information you're giving them is correct. They also have to trust that you won't share information that you don't have the ability to check, such as rumors and unfounded suspicions.

Your responsibility as a journalist is to prioritize accuracy in your work. Ethically, you're held to a higher standard than the average person sharing information on the internet, bloggers, or gossip sites. When you put the weight of journalism behind a story you share, you're telling audiences that this work is of the highest standard.

Getting Everything Right While Working

The first line of defense in avoiding factual errors is to develop a process that helps you record facts accurately in the first place. It doesn't mean that you don't have to check each fact later — you absolutely still need to do that process. But being thorough early on helps to prevent some mistakes in advance.

The seemingly simple directive to be accurate in your reporting can feel overwhelming, though. Identifying key opportunities to double-check your work helps because it allows you to think through the specific ways you can make mistakes — and those mistakes can grow into large errors.

Verifying during interviews

During the interview process, you have the opportunity to speak with your sources directly. So, it's the perfect time to ask for some initial clarification.

Here are some things you should learn to question and verify during the interview:

- **How to spell names and places:** Misspellings are some of the most common types of factual errors. And when you make them, you generally make them repeatedly throughout the story. It's a good practice to always confirm, for example, how a source spells their name, how their title or occupation should be explained, and what their pronouns are during the interview. It's always possible that it could be misspelled elsewhere, and you don't want to repeat that same mistake.

- **Numbers and statistics:** Any facts that have to do with numbers can be tricky. But you don't have to rely only on your own knowledge of the content matter. Especially when you're interviewing experts like scientists and researchers, you may want to verify that you're properly reading and interpreting the numbers and statistics you've pulled from their research.
- **Ideas you came into the interview with:** When you reach out to sources, you already have an idea in your head about what you think their contribution to your story will be and what their perspectives are. So, it's essential to confirm those assumptions because even assumptions that come from research should still be verified.
- **What they said in the interview:** As sources answer your questions, it's okay to confirm that you're understanding their answers correctly along the way. Not only does it help you when it's time to write your story later, but it also shows your source that you care about accurately representing what they're telling you.

The audience never hears from the source directly. It hears from the source through you — through the direct quotes you choose to include, through your paraphrasing of their thoughts, and through your presentation of them. So, it's important that you get it right.

Recording and transcribing

When you interview sources, recording the interviews to transcribe later is the key to accuracy. On occasion, a source sharing sensitive information or someone who may not want to be identified may not consent to being recorded. But generally, it's best practice to record every interview.

TIP

Here are some tips for doing this recording and then transcribing it afterward:

- **Request permission.** Although recording laws vary by state and can change, it's still best practice to always ask permission from a source to record.
- **Repeat that you are recording.** After hitting the Record button, mention again to your source that you're recording. It can be a simple, "Okay, so I'm now recording," to get the confirmation on tape.
- **Get spellings on tape.** Before you forget, get your source to spell their name on tape. That way, you can always fact-check yourself easily later.
- **Don't interrupt.** If possible, try your best not to interrupt your source when they're talking. This helps the recording have clear breaks between speakers and will help with transcription later.
- **Start your transcription.** Today, most journalists use one of many artificial intelligence (AI) tools for transcription. They aren't perfect, but they are a way to start your transcription because they pull in a lot of the wording for you and give you a great starting point. If you don't want to start with a transcription service, you can start by *logging your tape* (writing down the subjects of the conversation along with the corresponding time codes on the tape).
- **Clean up your transcription.** After you have a start to your transcription and you've listened again to your recording in some way, go through and clean up the AI transcription or type up the actual transcription into your tape log. Give priority to the quotes you think you'll use, and make sure you're spelling everything accurately and choosing the best punctuation to reflect how the interviewee spoke their sentences.

TIP

If there is ever a part of the audio recording that is unintelligible, note that in the transcription. Never put words in the source's mouth or paraphrase something you can't hear. It's essential to be true to what was said in the interview and never infer what a source meant.

Cross-checking sources

After you start to work on your story, it's important to continue to cross-check the facts that your sources gave you.

Here are some of the best and easiest resources for fact-checking at this stage:

- **Your transcript:** The transcript from your interview is always a good start. Here, you can reference exactly what the source said and how to confirm that you've explained it to the best of your ability.
- **Work websites:** Work websites can be helpful for a lot of detail, such as titles and information about products. However, you want to make sure that the information you see is current. For example, if a person's title is listed on their work website, it's best to confirm that it's still correct — sometimes there's a lag between organizational staffing changes and the updating of websites. Websites also often house other information (such as past press releases, photos and videos, and links to past work) that you can view.
- **LinkedIn and other social media sites:** Different social media sites are the home for different information. But LinkedIn (`www.linkedin.com`) is generally where people keep their work information updated, so it's a good place to verify information such as employment and education. Other social media sites may have this information listed as well, but not all people see places like Facebook and Instagram as places to accurately fill out that kind of information and keep it updated.

Although LinkedIn is a place that even employers consider pretty trustworthy, remember that people manually update their pages themselves and there are no checks and balances to prevent any exaggerating or even lying.

- **Other research and studies:** Unless your story is about someone's groundbreaking, new research, there should be other research that supports it. Even then, new discoveries are also built on prior studies. This is especially important in health and science reporting.

» **Other journalism articles:** When you refer to other journalism articles as a second source, you aren't "stealing" other journalists' reporting. You're using it to confirm that you're on the right track and that what people have told you aligns with prior reporting.

TIP

If you're interviewing a source who's in the media a lot, you probably won't be able to find every single journalism story they've been interviewed for, but try to at least look for recent stories and stories that specifically align with the topic your story is about.

Finishing Up Correctly

Finishing up your story provides another time to check your facts. It's when your story has all the facts that it will likely have, barring any last-minute changes or fixes.

WARNING

Errors are commonly added to stories during the editing process. So, it's really important to continue the fact-checking process and not assume that you've already checked everything.

Knowing what should be fact-checked

Especially in longer stories, thinking about everything you need to check can be overwhelming. So, how do you define what's a fact in a story, when in journalism, *everything* is pretty much based on facts?

In addition to the spellings of names and other proper nouns, here are some facts to easily identify:

» **Ages:** Ages are a common error in stories because people get older and have birthdays. Sources can be technically a year older by the time a story is published.

TIP

When you're interviewing for a story that you know will take weeks or months to report, don't just ask your sources for their ages. Also, ask them for their birth dates. This will avoid the need to call them back and ask them if they're still that age before publication.

- **Dates:** A typo in a date gives that date an entirely different meaning. For example, if an event happened in 1969, as opposed to accidentally typing that it occurred in 1996, that mistake is no longer a simple typo that the audience can easily decipher as an error.
- **Money:** You know to double-check your math because it's easy to let a small mistake give you extremely incorrect answers in a calculation (see Chapter 8). But making mistakes such as mixing up if something is millions or billions of dollars is also easy. It's a single-letter difference, but it has a major consequence in understanding.
- **Locations:** You may easily know if something happened in a major metro area. But mistakes often occur when journalists don't double-check boundaries to see the exact city or neighborhood where something took place before they add it to their stories. Know what that area is colloquially called, too. For example, it may be common practice to call a small city or town a suburb of a larger city in one metro area, but it may be more common to refer to the county in another. Chicago media refers to places right outside of the city as suburban, such as suburban Oak Park, while the Atlanta area has more unincorporated neighborhoods on its outskirts, so its media would refer to many areas by their county names.
- **Opinions:** You're interviewing people and sharing their opinions. So, don't forget that those opinions are facts, too. You want to confirm both the source's actual opinions and any basis for those opinions.
- **Captions:** Many people forget about captions because photos, videos, maps, charts, and graphs may not be added to the story until the very end of the process. But audiences will assume that the information in captions has also been fact-checked and is correct — and it should be.

TIP

All stories are different, and you may realize that you have a different list of common facts that you don't want to forget in your stories. Make a checklist of the types of facts you want to be able to check every single time, and stick to it.

Referring to interview tape

So, you have your interview tape, as well as your transcription or tape log. But the recording won't be as helpful as it can be if you don't set it up in the best way to help you in your workflow. The key is to go back and identify what you'll need to be able to easily access to fact-check.

Here are some ways to ensure you can refer to your interview tape as you need to:

- **Mark it with software.** AI transcription tools allow you to add notes and highlight parts of your audio. This will help you play certain points of the tape without having to scroll through it.
- **Type it in your log.** Even if you don't use any tools, you can easily go back to your tape log and add more details for facts you'll want to verify later. Just add the time on the recording and the fact (for example, "0:22 — name spelling and title").
- **Write it down in a notebook.** Even with all the tools available, some people still prefer to write everything down with pen and paper. It's why you'll rarely catch a journalist without a notebook! So, feel free to keep it simple if you don't want to use electronics.

REMEMBER

The recording is only as good as what you can hear to confirm yourself, without making assumptions. When you're using the interview tape to fact-check, you're only verifying facts that the source said directly. Don't infer anything the source did not explicitly state. Making assumptions is one reason why you can fact-check and still have errors.

Calling sources back

Calling sources back to check facts is an essential and important part of fact-checking. It really ensures that your sources are in the know about what you're reporting. This doesn't mean that you're explaining everything that's in your story — in fact, you *shouldn't* share your stories with your sources before publication. You can and should, however, confirm with them what they said so that they can confirm and verify it.

Here are some tips for when it's time to call your sources back to do a fact-check:

- **To confirm easy facts:** Get easy facts out of the way by asking about those first. Check them off as you ask them.
- **To verify ideas:** Ideas are more difficult to confirm, so take your time and carefully ask about them. Some helpful language in asking those questions could be:
  - "Is it accurate to say that you believe . . ."
  - "Would you say that . . ."
  - "Is it fair to say . . ."
- **Ask if anything has changed:** If there are specific parts of your story that are timely, specifically ask questions about them. But you can also just ask: "Have there been any changes since we last spoke?"

TIP

Putting time in with your sources to fact-check not only results in a stronger story but also shows your sources that you're committed to being a professional and helps build trust with them. This can be extra helpful if you need to interview them again in the future.

Finding reinforcement

You're ultimately responsible for fact-checking your own work — when mistakes happen, it's your name on the byline. But you should lean on the help of others when available, and for high-stakes stories — stories in which getting facts incorrect can have grave consequences — draw upon every resource available to ensure you're on track.

Here are some of the people to call for reinforcement:

- **Colleagues:** Your colleagues want to help, and you can and should return the favor for them.
- **Editors:** Your editors are a great line of defense because as they edit your work for structure and clarity, they also may point out a fact that looks off or something else that could use checking.
- **Copy editors:** Not all organizations use copy editors today, but they're essential in fact-checking, especially for daily news and shorter stories.
- **Fact-checkers:** For big stories especially, fact-checkers can step in and do a formal fact-check (which entails checking every single fact in your story) after your story is completed.

TIP

Working as a fact-checker used to be a good way to get a foot in the door, especially in the magazine industry. Although many places no longer employ full-time fact-checkers, they still hire them on a contract basis. Being a fact-checker allows you to meet editors, show your skills, and make money while you're at it.

Annotating a Finished Story

Whether you have the benefit of an official fact-checker or not, the full fact-checking process is one that is extremely beneficial and entails annotating a story after it's complete.

Here's how to do it:

1. **Mark up each fact in the story so that it's clear what you'll be checking on.**

   Traditionally, fact-checkers would print out stories and underline each fact. If you're fact-checking digitally, you can use the highlight feature to highlight each fact, change the font color, or use the underline tool.

2. **Look for the facts that are the easiest to verify first.**

   For example, maybe you can confirm the spelling of something a source sent you in an email.

3. **Go through interview transcripts and recordings for further clarification.**

4. **Contact sources to verify the rest.**

   This may also mean contacting people who you didn't interview but who can help (for example, calling the administrative assistant of a CEO to verify the CEO's previous job title).

TIP

Calling people on the phone is usually best for fact-checking, especially if you're fact-checking more than a couple of details. However, if you need to ask a short follow-up question, like to confirm someone's age, an email is generally okay.

Making Corrections

Making corrections is a key part of journalism transparency. When you make a mistake, you want your audience to know that you've acknowledged it and fixed it. No matter how well you fact-check, corrections still happen. So, your goal should be to do them to the highest of standards.

What can and cannot be ethically corrected

Although you want to correct anything that is incorrect in your story, there are some instances when a change or correction may be requested, but you're unable to do so ethically.

Here are some guiding principles around ethical corrections:

- **Don't change what a source actually said.** Sometimes, a source will request that you edit what they said because they don't like how they said it. Maybe they feel they didn't sound eloquent enough or maybe they just think they could have said it better. Regardless of the reason, you can't change those things. You can, however, talk to the source about whether there is a way to add a clarification to the story because your goal is to make sure your audience understands what the source said.

- **Listen to requests for corrections and concerns about mistakes.** This doesn't mean that you should automatically make a change. But you should look into whether you made a mistake and bring in other points of view within the newsroom, if possible, to help you determine if you should edit anything.
- **You can make corrections on any platform.** Treat every place you share information — social media included — as a place where an error can occur. So, in that vein, you need to have processes for issuing corrections everywhere.

TIP

With corrections, time is of the essence. Try to slow down and evaluate the mistake, see if there are any additional mistakes, and then make the correction. There are few things more embarrassing than needing to make continued corrections on the same story due to carelessness.

Who is responsible for fixing mistakes

Ultimately, fixing mistakes is your responsibility. It's not something you just pass on to your editor for someone else to handle. So, it's important to have a good grasp on understanding the mistakes you make.

TIP

Here are some ways to avoid having errors in your stories:

- **Slow down.** Even if you write fast, edit (and fact-check) slowly.
- **Know yourself.** Learn what your common mistakes are. Then give extra attention to fact-checking.
- **Avoid multitasking.** When going through a story, try to read one thing at a time. For example, read through it just for typos, and then read through it again to check for name misspellings.

When you know what the mistake is, gather all the information needed. There are two parts to a correction: the actual correction you make and the note of the correction. Depending on your newsroom, your editor or another colleague — for example, a digital editor who runs the website — may need to make the actual change after you've written the update.

Even if it's commonplace in your newsroom for someone else to publish the correction, knowing exactly what it should be and how it should be explained helps make the process smoother for everyone and avoids further mistakes.

How to make corrections with transparency

The second part of the correction is where or how you explain to audiences what the mistake is. This is key. Every journalism organization has slightly different language for writing these corrections, but here is some of the writing you may see:

- **Editor's note:** An editor's note can be added to a story for many reasons, such as to add clarifying information about the story or explain the reasoning behind something.
- **Clarification:** Sometimes you aren't correcting something that was wrong but just adding additional context to make its meaning clearer. This often indicates that there is clarifying information within the story itself (not just in a note).
- **Correction:** Corrections are often used when you want to be extremely clear that something was incorrect and has now been corrected. This statement may use terms like *incorrectly stated, misstated,* and *wrongly reported.*
- **Retraction:** Retractions are extremely rare. But if a story is deemed too inaccurate to fix and must be retracted, it's removed and replaced with a retraction. This note may be a simple line, or it may go deep into detail about why the story was retracted.

The key to writing a good correction of any kind is to be clear and straightforward in your wording. Don't try to downplay the mistake. Keep it simple.

3 Working within the Bounds of Ethics and the Law

IN THIS PART . . .

Consider the journalism code of ethics and the ethical responsibility journalism entails.

Learn the legal protections and rights you have as a journalist.

Examine artificial intelligence, its growth, and its new role in journalism — including its many ethical challenges and considerations.

IN THIS CHAPTER

» Understanding the importance of ethical standards

» Using a code of ethics in your work

Chapter 10 Getting Clear on the Journalism Code of Ethics

Journalism ethics is one of the most talked about parts of the job. That's because it governs every single thing you do as a journalist. All the different practices and norms that have worked their way into how journalists talk to people and report on issues should align with these ethical standards.

In this chapter, I discuss how journalism ethics come into play in your work and the common standards all journalists follow.

Knowing Why Journalists Should Abide by a Code

Before becoming a journalist, I didn't fully understand why journalists should abide by an ethical code. I didn't see journalism as being different than most other industries, and I falsely assumed that as long as I was an ethical person, I would be an ethical journalist.

After actually joining the field, though, I soon learned just how nuanced being a journalist can be. It's a huge responsibility, and that's because journalists have a huge platform to spread information. In doing so, we can be helpful or harmful. Journalists are accountable to the public and must think not only about their day-to-day work, but also about how even the smallest decisions impact the greater good. Having a code of ethics helps journalists ensure they're meeting that goal.

In this section, I walk you through why such a code is essential in how it affects journalists' work and how people trust it.

Considering journalists' responsibility to inform the public

As journalists, our charge is to inform the public about everything that is going on around us. To do this, there are some ethical considerations to keep in mind:

- **Journalism has competition from other types of media.** Not only do people get information from journalism mediums such as newspapers, TV, and radio, but they also get it from places like blogs, non-journalism podcasts, and social media gossip accounts. Ethical codes help journalists to establish a standard that differentiates themselves from others.
- **There is a lot of wrong information in the world.** Because there are so many places to get information, it can be overwhelming for people to wade through it all. You want to establish that your work is accurate and truthful and can be trusted.
- **You shouldn't just be talking *at* audiences.** You engage with the public by working with them and listening to them. That's how you understand their needs better.

REMEMBER

Today, the places that journalists use to disseminate information are the same places some people use to share *misinformation* (information that is factually incorrect), *disinformation* (information that is incorrect and used to deceive people), and *malinformation* (information that was once true but is used to cause harm).

Recognizing the importance of audience trust

Audience trust is essential. You can do an awesome job of reporting a story, but if the public doesn't trust what you publish, then you haven't done your job.

Here are some things to keep in mind while building audience trust:

- **Past experience matters.** People take into account if you've been accurate and fair in the past. If they think a journalism organization has a history of poor practices, they won't trust what that organization produces now — even if it *is* accurate. If you work at such an organization, your own credibility could be on the line, so be wary of working somewhere that isn't trustworthy.
- **You have to listen.** Audiences tell you when they don't understand something or when they think you've done something wrong. You have to be open to listening to that feedback and having a real dialogue with them about the decisions you make and whether you should modify your practices.
- **Building trust has to be an everyday goal.** The small, everyday decisions you make are the ones that have the largest impact on trust. So, it's not enough to think about trust only for huge stories. You also gain your audience's trust with daily stories, how you post on social media, the headlines you write, and the photos you choose for stories. All these tiny decisions affect trust.

TIP

Put yourself in the shoes of the various people in your audience. For example, if you're a local reporter, will people on a certain side of the city be upset at a list of "best restaurants" that totally ignores them? Seeing your story from the perspective of the various members of your audience is critical because trust can be eroded if you don't.

Identifying Common Principles across Codes of Ethics

Many journalism organizations exist, each with its own set of specific rules. In fact, every newsroom you work in will have its own ethical handbook. But there are some large, general principles that are standard across the industry. You can find these principles in almost every code of ethics.

Truthfulness and accuracy

As a journalist, your work must be true and accurate. That means:

- **The facts and information are gathered in a way that leads to accuracy.** You asked the right people the right questions in the news-gathering process.
- **You spend time checking your facts and ensuring that the final story is right.** The fact-checking process is just as important as everything else. And rushing is not an excuse to be incorrect.
- **You work to make sure there is no ambiguity in what things mean.** You use clarity to ensure context and meanings aren't misconstrued in your stories.

Impartiality and fairness

Impartiality and fairness are tied to truthfulness and accuracy: Audiences won't believe your work is true if they think you weren't fair in how you completed it.

Here's what impartiality and fairness mean in ethics:

- **You aren't partial to anything but the truth.** To be fair, you give everyone the chance to be heard.
- **You think about your biases.** Everyone has biases, so you should understand yours so you can acknowledge them and be fair even to people you don't agree with.
- **The appearance of being partial sometimes means just as much to audiences.** If you're being impartial but your audience thinks you're not, they'll lose trust in you and the work you produce.

WARNING

The idea of "fake news" sometimes stems from the thinking that journalists' work isn't trustworthy because it's not impartial. This idea is often manipulated by those with bad intentions to erode the public's trust in media completely.

Independence

The term *independent journalist* means a journalist who doesn't work for an organization and is working and publishing stories on their own. But in the case of ethics, *independence* means something quite different. Independence has to do with a journalist or media organization being independent of any outside influences that could dictate what they report on and how they report.

Here's what independence looks like:

- **No government agency is involved.** Holding the government accountable is how journalism supports democracy. So, it can have no hand in dictating what's covered in a newsroom and what isn't.
- **No major corporation is paying for coverage.** Media organizations are businesses, and they need money to run. That money is often earned through advertising. Even in the case of nonprofits, organizations are given grants from major philanthropy organizations and use underwriting to pay for editorial projects such as podcasts. However, these organizations have no control over what's produced.

» **The business side of a newsroom is not involved in editorial decisions.** To ensure that a newsroom's coverage is not influenced by its business needs, most places draw very clear and distinct lines between those raising the money and those working on the news. They do this to avoid any intentional or unintentional influences.

Looking at the Society of Professional Journalists Code of Ethics

The Society of Professional Journalists (SPJ) has created a code of ethics that sets the standard for journalists in a wide range of disciplines. This code is the most widely accepted code for journalists in the United States, and it's often referenced, pulled from, and adapted. SPJ also ensures that this code is up-to-date based on what's currently happening around the world, so it's trusted by journalists everywhere.

In the area of ethics, SPJ has identified four major areas for journalistic standards: telling the truth, minimizing harm, being independent, and being transparent.

TIP

In addition to its work around ethics, SPJ is an advocacy organization that you can join. Membership in such organizations is helpful for everyone, but journalists who are newer to the industry often find it helps them make meaningful connections with other people. Head to `www.spj.org` for more information.

TIP

You can read the SPJ Code of Ethics in full at `www.spj.org/ethicscode.asp`.

Seeking truth and reporting it

The first area in the SPJ Code of Ethics emphasizes how journalists' work should be grounded in the truth and also how you should be "honest and courageous" in what you do. This means:

- You're responsible for making sure the stories you put out are accurate.
- Not only do you ensure accuracy in the details of a story, but you also ensure that you aren't misrepresenting the truth in any way.
- Who you talk to is important, and you should make clear to your audience who your sources are and what their individual motivations are.
- You should be checking your own biases at all times. And you should be clearly labeling any opinion stories as such so it's clear to your audience that opinion stories are different from other journalism stories.

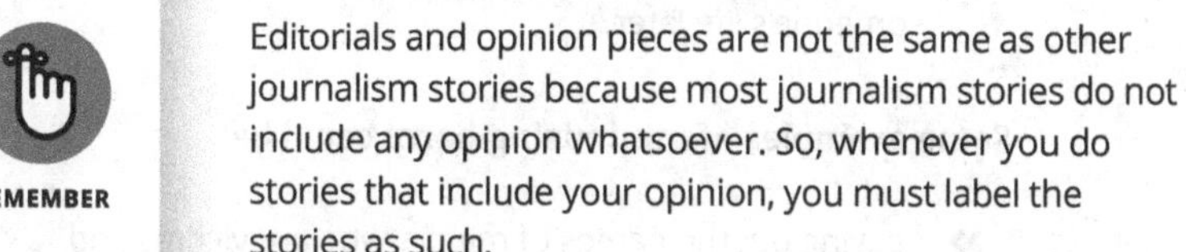

Editorials and opinion pieces are not the same as other journalism stories because most journalism stories do not include any opinion whatsoever. So, whenever you do stories that include your opinion, you must label the stories as such.

- Your job is to hold people in power accountable. Stories that shed light on the things people want to keep under wraps do that.

Some examples of seeking the truth could be:

- Updating a breaking news story with new facts and information
- Uncovering an unlawful use of government funds
- Reaching out to a source for comment when they're accused of something

Regardless of the person or organization, *always* try to seek comment from those who are being accused of any wrongdoing in your stories. You should give them the opportunity to respond before a story is published.

Minimizing harm

Minimizing harm involves thinking through how you treat people, including the sources you interview directly, any other people or organizations you talk about in your stories, members of the public in general, and your own colleagues. This means:

- You think about what information must be shared and how it may impact others. If there's a potential negative impact, you have to try your best to minimize this.
- You should prioritize the needs of vulnerable groups during reporting. You should work to not re-traumatize people.
- In crime stories, you should balance what details are necessary to share because the public needs to know them with the potential to cause harm to a suspect's right to a fair trial.
- Think about how what you publish today may affect someone's life later.

Some examples of minimizing harm could be:

- Leaving out the names of minors who are victims and, sometimes, the names of their parents if it would easily identify them
- Not publishing mug shots of everyone accused of a crime because they haven't been tried in a court of law yet
- Withholding information found in a court document that's not necessary to tell a story

WARNING

You may be so anxious to publish everything that you know in a story that you don't stop to think about why those details are included and if they're needed. Slow down and take a breath to think through anything that could cause harm. Sometimes those details aren't needed for a robust, accurate, and fair story anyway.

Acting independently

Working independently of any outside influences is essential in getting and keeping the public's trust. This means:

- You not only avoid conflicts of interest but also ensure that there is no appearance of influence from an outside party that would affect your ability to report fairly.

» You never ever accept payment for news coverage. No exceptions.

» If an outlet has ads or any type of paid content, it's clearly labeled as such.

Acting independently could look like:

» Not accepting expensive gifts from any person or organization you could potentially report on in the future

» Using special music in a podcast to indicate something is an ad

» Not mixing sponsored content with journalistic stories

» Not using a source that offered money (even if you don't accept it — and you obviously shouldn't!)

REMEMBER

Trust is everything with your audience. So, acting independently is also about the appearance of bias or influence. Avoid any potential issues.

Being accountable and transparent

Being accountable and transparent in journalism is about taking responsibility for your own work and also being open to sharing with your audiences the decisions you make before, during, and after the reporting process. This means:

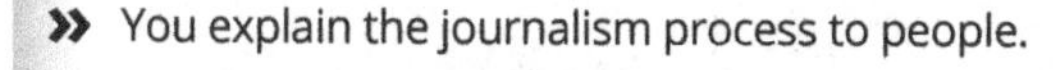

» You explain the journalism process to people.

REMEMBER

Take extra care in explaining the journalism process to sources. Unless someone is interviewed often by the media, they likely don't understand all the ins and outs of how a story comes together. These details also vary by journalism organization, so it's always helpful to ensure your sources know what's happening throughout the process.

» Don't ignore people's concerns about your coverage. Instead, address those concerns.

- Engage with your audience to create a dialogue about what you're doing and why. This kind of dialogue allows them to also share their thoughts.
- Hold yourself accountable for what you publish and anything that happens because of it.
- Hold your fellow journalists accountable — and expect the same from them. You and your fellow journalists are all one industry, and the general public views you as such. It's important that you also expect the highest standards from each other.

Being accountable and transparent could look like:

- Accepting responsibility for an error
- Deleting a social media post and resharing it with a correction
- Writing a post about why you and your newsroom made a certain editorial decision
- Engaging in a discussion with community members on how they'd like to see a certain type of story handled in the future

IN THIS CHAPTER

» Recognizing a journalist's privilege

» Accessing trials and courts

» Learning about Freedom of Information Act requests

Chapter 11 Knowing Your Rights as a Journalist

Just you need to pay attention to your responsibility as a journalist, you need to know that you also have rights to help you uphold these principles. As the "fourth estate," journalism supports democracy, and because of this, journalists have to have legal rights that support the work they do.

The term *fourth estate* refers to how journalism fits within — or alongside — the three branches of government. The U.S. Constitution outlines the legislative branch (Congress), the executive branch (the president, vice president, and cabinet), and the judicial branch (the Supreme Court and other federal courts). The press is seen as an unofficial fourth branch within this system. That's because it helps keep a balance of power by ensuring that people in these positions of power are monitored and held accountable. Journalism's work as a government watchdog is just as essential as having each of the three branches balance each other's power.

In addition to protecting free speech, the First Amendment of the U.S. Constitution protects press freedom. *Press freedom* may be defined in many ways, but a good way to think about it is as an opening for allowing journalists to do their jobs uninterrupted. For example, so many of journalists' legal rights and protections have to do with one of the hardest things of the job — access. This includes access to:

- Press conferences
- Documents
- Certain spaces such as courtrooms
- Records that are not publicly shared
- Government officials

These laws exist so journalists are legally protected when they're reporting and so both they and their work have some safeguards.

In this chapter, I cover your rights as a journalist and how to access them. I also help you understand the legal limitations to privileges.

Understanding Your Rights as a Journalist to Cover the Government

Journalists' responsibility is to cover the government. So, they must have some protections in order to do their job. And although there are some things anyone can do, journalists need what is considered by most courts an extra privilege (often called *journalist's privilege* or *reporter's privilege*).

Here are some of the things that constitute this privilege for journalists under the First Amendment:

- **Interview notes and recordings:** You may think that your notes and recordings from your interviews are automatically private, but that's not true. It's journalist's privilege that protects this privacy in most cases.

- **Anonymous sources:** Have you ever heard a journalist in a movie say: "I'll never give up my sources"? When you promise to protect the identity of a source, it's this kind of privilege that's your legal argument if law enforcement tries to force you to tell them who your sources are when you've promised them anonymity.

When you promise anonymity to a source, you should be willing to be arrested or face any other kind of intimidation to protect it. Of course, this is likely only an issue in very rare stories, but it's essential to understand that you're assuming a level of risk every time you agree to anonymous sources. It's another reason why it's helpful to work with a trusted editor.

- **Confidential documents:** Similar to source interviews, you may obtain documents that you need to keep confidential. You can argue privilege to try to keep them safe.
- **Testifying in court:** You may be called to court to testify against sources or about your reporting. You may be able to use privilege to prevent yourself from having to testify, especially in regard to reporting that was never released to the public.

Privilege for journalists looks very different in every state. It's important to know what it means where you're working and look up recent cases surrounding privilege in case it has changed because it's up to the courts' interpretation of the First Amendment.

Journalist's privilege makes sense. It allows you to do your job better. Just think about how it often allows for the following cases:

- Getting firsthand witness accounts who want to be anonymous to protect their safety
- Reporting and releasing documents that show government wrongdoing
- Consistently covering protests and civil unrest

Even though it is illegal to do so, many journalists may be arrested while doing their jobs. For example, while covering protests, journalists are often arrested. You may have even seen it captured on TV.

Wearing your press badge (which identifies you and what media outlet you work for) is always helpful, but it's extra helpful in these instances. On the back of that badge or within its sleeve, add any necessary numbers such as that of your newsroom editor or your organization's legal team. Although it may not prevent an arrest, it can help in ensuring you can quickly access the help you need.

When you think about why your rights as a journalist are so important, it's helpful to remember that not every journalist around the world has such protections.

Here are some common global issues that freedom of the press aims to solve:

- **Information suppression:** In some places, information is not allowed to be shared with the public. Not only can journalists not be government watchdogs, but their governments control what is published and only state-sanctioned media are allowed.
- **Arrests and imprisonment:** In some countries, journalists are often arrested for doing what journalists in the United States do every single day. And they often don't have legal arguments to fight against those arrests
- **Physical danger and harm:** Not all militaries respect press vests. Especially in areas of war, journalists lose their lives reporting.

Covering Trials and Courts

One really important area of journalists' access is to trials and courts. This is because of journalism's essential role in informing the public. In this section, I guide you through how to cover them.

Official proceedings

Journalists are able to cover hearings and trials, even when the general public cannot. But it's important to note that there are times when a journalist's privilege is not recognized in official proceedings:

- **Absolute versus qualified privilege:** Some states have *absolute privilege,* where the idea of privilege applies to anyone who fits its definition of a journalist. Other states have *qualified privilege,* which is conditional and only applies in certain situations.
- **Full-time journalist's versus nontraditional journalist's privilege:** Some states also make a distinction between journalists who work full-time at major news organizations and journalists who may freelance, work for their own publications, or work at lesser-known places.

Official proceedings can also be closed to both the public and journalists. They can be closed for the following reasons:

- **For privacy:** Especially in dangerous cases, a court proceeding may be closed to protect the privacy and identity of victims or witnesses — or sometimes even jurors.
- **To protect a defendant's rights:** Courts may decide to close a proceeding to ensure that a defendant has the right to a fair trial and that the jury is impartial.
- **To protect youth:** In the case of juvenile proceedings, there is no right to access. When a person under 18 is on trial for a serious crime, such as murder, some states do allow people, including journalists, in the courtroom with the argument that the public has a reasonable interest in knowing what's happening.

Court records

For court proceedings that are public, their accompanying records are usually public — or become public at some point. This includes documents such as:

- Court transcripts

- Evidence introduced at trial
- Filings
- Judgments
- Jury records
- Witness lists

Journalists can find most court records using Public Access to Court Electronic Records (PACER; `https://pacer.uscourts.gov`). Most newsrooms have a PACER subscription in order to have this access available at all times.

However, if you're looking for an older court record — likely anything before 1999 — you'll need to contact the court where the record originated. Some of these older documents may have been transferred to the National Archives and Records Administration (NARA), but many no longer exist. (Before court records were online, they were kept only for a period of time and periodically destroyed.)

However, documents that are sealed or that were a part of a closed hearing are not available to the public.

Accessing Government Documents through the Freedom of Information Act

Outside of accessing court documents, journalists work hard to get access to other kinds of government records. Sometimes, the key to finding these is just knowing where to look.

REMEMBER

Websites for cities, counties, states, and the federal government often report certain information on a monthly, quarterly, or annual basis.

But when the information you're seeking isn't easily shared, journalists often know how to submit specific requests for them.

Understanding the law

In order to access open records, there is a very essential law on your side as a journalist: the Freedom of Information Act (FOIA). FOIA (pronounced *foy*-uh) gives anyone in the public the right to request records from federal agencies. FOIA has been in place since 1967, and it's meant to help the everyday citizen know what government agencies are doing.

FOIA is a law that journalists often employ, but *anyone* can use it. That means that there is no special certification needed to file an open-records request, often just called a FOIA request. Absolutely anyone can submit a request.

Here are some basic facts about FOIA:

- **It's recognized by all three branches of the government.** Congress, the president, and the Supreme Court all recognize FOIA.
- **Each agency handles its own FOIA requests.** There is no one place that accepts all open-records requests. Instead, each agency has its own office that does so.
- **FOIA law is for requesting information that agencies already have.** FOIA requests can't ask agencies to create new records that they don't already have.

In the following sections, I guide you through FOIA law and how to use it. I also talk about how to handle roadblocks and explain the law's limitations.

What the law says

FOIA is a lengthy piece of legislation — one that has been amended and changed since it was first enacted. Let me break down some of what the act's text actually says:

- Agencies must publish where the public can make open-records requests and who handles them.
- The instructions for making the requests must be shared.
- Agencies can redact identifying information from the records they release to protect people's privacy.

» If it's possible to do so, agencies should provide the records in the formats in which they're requested. (For example, if a person requests a spreadsheet, and the data is available in a spreadsheet, the public information officer should send a spreadsheet instead of a PDF.)

» Agencies have to make a "reasonable effort" to search for the information requested.

» Agencies can also charge fees for some reasons (for example, if fulfilling the request requires a lot of manpower).

» Agencies have 20 days to determine if they can fulfill requests, and requesters have 90 days to appeal any decision from an agency that says they cannot.

The "presumption of openness"

The idea of "presumption of openness" is part of FOIA law, and it's a beneficial one for journalists. It means that agencies should approach FOIA requests in an attempt to give requesters as much information as possible.

In 2022, new FOIA guidelines around this idea further emphasized these foundational ideas:

» **FOIA requests are an essential tool in democracy.** Allowing individual citizens the opportunity to view open records helps them understand the government, and it should be seen as a necessity.

» **Transparency should be a top goal.** The point of FOIA requests is to give people access to documents they otherwise wouldn't be able to see. So, the goal should not be to try to hide these records but to make every attempt to fulfill requests.

» **A "spirit of cooperation" should be part of effective communication.** Public information officers at agencies should work with people who make FOIA requests, responding promptly, providing updates, and keeping them informed of the progress of their requests.

Who issues guidance to agencies

Although agencies are responsible for fulfilling their own requests, standards must be in place for the FOIA process. The Office of Information Policy at the Department of Justice issues guidance to agencies. This guidance is:

- Government-wide, affecting all U.S. agencies
- A means of compliance, giving agencies clearly defined responsibilities
- In the spirit of FOIA, encouraging transparency and openness

TIP

The best starting point for reading more about FOIA requests is `www.foia.gov`. From there, you can use search tools to help you find what may already be available. The website also has another search tool to help specifically with your request by giving you all the information you'll need to contact your intended agency, including who is working there as FOIA officers.

Making a request

The process of making an open-records request may feel intimidating if you've never done it before.

The Office of Information Policy explains the process of making a FOIA request in the following simple steps:

1. **Do your research.**

   Researching exactly what you want to get from your FOIA request is helpful in ensuring you receive what you need. Sometimes it can even be the difference in your receiving anything at all.

2. **Find the right agency.**

   Multiple agencies could have the information you need. Save time by figuring out which agency to send your request to before blindly sending off a request.

3. **Submit your request.**

   After you submit your request, the agency makes its determination. The agency has to figure out what information it can share before fulfilling your request.

In the following sections, I cover what you'll need to make your own FOIA request.

What kinds of documents you can ask for

Although people often think of documents as those that can be printed on paper, the kinds of records you can request through a FOIA request are wide-ranging, including the following:

- Documents and reports
- Emails
- Text messages (on phones used for work)
- Closed-circuit television (CCTV) footage
- Photographs

The different processes of different agencies

Although there is a single piece of legislation that governs all FOIA requests and standardized guidance issued by the Office of Information Policy, there are still many ways agencies can fulfill requests. It's one of the reasons why performing research is so essential.

Here are some differences to keep in mind:

- **There is no specific form.** Although some of the standard information you should include in FOIA requests may be similar, there is no form that you can use for every agency.
- **Categories can be called different things across agencies.** Remember that you want to make your request as specific as possible, and to do that, you'll want to use the same language that that particular agency uses. For

example, a field titled *ticketer* in a database for one agency may be titled *resident* in another.

REMEMBER

Logs of previous FOIA requests may be available. Viewing those logs can help you properly formulate the request so you know what categories are available.

- **Different FOIA officers may have different preferences.** At the end of the day, FOIAs are handled by people.

FOIA officers and how to find them

Building relationships with FOIA or public information officers is helpful. These are the people who are assisting you, so it's helpful to be kind and respectful in your communication with them — just as you would with anyone else.

To find an agency's FOIA officer, check the following:

- **The agency's website:** Go to the agency's site and look for "FOIA" or "public information officer" guidelines.
- **The FOIA website:** Go to `www.foia.gov`, select the Create a Request tab, and search for the agency.

TIP

Because FOIA requests can sometimes be confusing, many journalism organizations offer free FOIA training that provides specific tips and tricks that can help. One tip I hear often: Get to know FOIA officers well!

Knowing the legal limitations

Although there is a lot you can do when it comes to accessing government documents, limitations still exist. There are nine exemptions to FOIA law, stating that agencies do not release information that is:

- Classified and protects the country's security
- About an agency's internal personnel rules
- Prohibited by other laws
- Confidential and financial such as trade secrets

- Privileged communications between agencies
- Harmful to an individual person's privacy
- Used by law enforcement and could interfere with that work
- About supervising financial institutions
- About the location of wells

TIP

You probably won't remember all nine exemptions, so think about them as groups. In summary, all nine exemptions can be categorized into three groups:

- **Personal privacy:** Keeping individual people's right to privacy
- **National security:** Keeping the country's right to safety
- **Law enforcement:** Keeping law enforcement's ability to solve cases unobstructed

In addition to these exemptions, there is a special protection known as *exclusions*. These three categories involve very specific situations, involving pending law enforcement proceedings, informant records, and Federal Bureau of Investigation (FBI) classified records.

Examples of FOIAs that may be denied include

- A FOIA requesting info about an ongoing criminal case
- A FOIA asking for info that would give a victim's name not yet shared publicly
- A FOIA requesting information about a person's firing

TIP

If your FOIA request is denied, think about the information that is truly important to your work and resubmit with the goal of avoiding information that may be unnecessary.

IN THIS CHAPTER

» Understanding the most common legal issues for journalists

» Knowing where to go for legal help

Chapter 12
Coping with Common Legal Considerations

Although journalists have many rights and protections, you can still get into legal trouble. Sometimes legal issues come from the government and its agencies; other times they come from private organizations, companies, and industries.

It's important to understand the many ways your work may be risky so that you can evaluate what resources you'll need. Thinking through this risk is especially important if you don't work at a large news organization with in-house legal counsel.

In this chapter, I fill you in on the most common legal problems that you could face as a journalist, suggest ways to avoid them, and share advice on where to look for help if you ever need it.

Identifying the Most Common Legal Issues Journalists Face

Journalists aren't lawyers, and it can be intimidating to think through all the possible ways you can get in legal trouble doing your job. But there are some very common issues that new journalists should learn about.

In the following sections, I walk you through the most common areas of legal trouble for journalists.

Privacy

As a journalist, your job is to look for people. In a way, and depending on the story, that may mean that you work harder than people in most industries to track people down and try to speak to them. However, there are lines that you shouldn't cross when it comes to privacy. And when you do cross them, you can get into legal trouble.

Generally, journalists shouldn't go against a person's reasonable expectation of privacy. Examples of acts that may fall into this area include:

- Using a hidden microphone or camera
- Sharing the private facts of ordinary citizens without cause
- Following someone into a place that most people would consider private such as a restroom (even if it's in a public place)

Trespassing

You always want to get as close as possible to the people who are part of your story. But you have to be careful when you're on private property — if you're asked to leave and you don't, you can be arrested for trespassing.

In public places (like on the street, in a park, or in a government building), the police may ask you to leave and may arrest you for trespassing if you don't — even if you *do* have a right to be there and you can make a strong case for it.

A press badge that identifies you and what media outlet you work for can be helpful if you're arrested. Even if the press badge doesn't prevent you from being arrested, it can help others around you who may be witnessing the arrest and it can provide quick access to any necessary numbers you may have on the back of the press badge, such as the number of your newsroom editor or your organization's legal team.

Copyright infringement

What you can and cannot publish in regards to others' property (such as images, videos, and even social media posts) can be tricky. Even when people give you permission to post things, there can be some confusion around who actually owns the rights to them.

For example, let's say you're writing a profile of a mayoral candidate, and the campaign gives you permission to use the photo of the candidate that's on the campaign website and all over the candidate's social media. Just because the photographer allowed them to use the photo for that reason doesn't mean the photo can be used as a press photo. Surprisingly, this is an issue that happens quite often, and it can cause a lot of confusion.

Copyright law is an important concept to understand in journalism because every journalist publishes their work somewhere, and sometimes it involves using the assets and resources created by others. Copyright infringement is how many newsrooms get in trouble — publishing things like photos and videos that they simply don't have the right to publish.

When you write something, take a photo, or create any other kind of work, it's automatically protected by copyright law. It only has to meet the following three criteria:

- **It's an original.** It shouldn't be copied from something else. This is a low threshold of creativity.

» **It's a work of authorship.** *Work of authorship* is just a legal category that includes forms of expression that can be protected by copyright law, such as literary, audiovisual, and sculptural works.

» **It's fixed.** It's not about to change again. For example, after you complete your poem, it's fixed.

Not only is *copyright infringement* (publishing things you don't have the right to publish) a huge ethical dilemma, but it's also an extremely costly one.

Many people know about *fair use* (the legal use of copyrighted work for freedom of expression), but it's often misinterpreted. Here are some common myths about fair use:

» **"I can use it as long as I attribute the author."** Just because you say who the author or owner is of the work doesn't mean you can use it.

» **"If it's on social media, then I can use it."** Many, many things are shared on social media by users who don't have the right to share them themselves.

» **"The copyright owner shared it publicly, so I can use it."** Even if the owner of the work shared it online, on social media, or anywhere else, that still doesn't give you the right to share it.

There is a common misconception that works such as photos that are shared online become okay for anyone to use. That's simply not the case. This thinking can be an extremely costly lesson for many journalists.

Thankfully, the U.S. Copyright Office has guidance on thinking through fair use. It's evaluated using the following four questions:

» **What is the purpose of using the work?** Some nonprofit educational and noncommercial uses are more likely to be considered fair use. This is also true if the work is *transformative,* which means it'll be changed to have a new purpose.

- **What is the nature of the work?** To support creative expression, more creative works (such as novels, art, and music) are more protected. Also, works that are not yet published are more protected so the creator has the right to publish them first.
- **How much of the work is used?** There is no set length that is fair use, but courts evaluate the quantity and quality of what will be used and it's proportional to the full work, with the goal not to use the "heart" of it.
- **What will the effects of using the work be?** If using part of the original work will negatively affect the work's market value, it may not be seen as fair use.

Using these factors, there are certain areas in which fair use is often granted:

- News reporting
- Criticism and commenting
- Teaching
- Scholarship and research

Examples of fair use could be:

- Using current videos on a late-night show
- Reproducing a photograph for a teaching presentation
- Quoting a short excerpt from a book in a review about it

In the following sections, I explain how to use written work, photographs, videos, and music and audio without getting into legal trouble.

Written work

Some types of journalism stories may require pulling in written work. For example, stories such as book reviews often use excerpts in order to discuss the work.

TIP

Here are some general best practices around using written work:

- **Use only what you need.** Quote from written work sparingly to be safe. Choose quotes that are strong and that best help show what you're discussing. For everything else, paraphrase. Lean into the strongest quotes that best demonstrate your points.
- **Attribute correctly.** Make sure that you're accurately attributing what excerpts are from the written work and what may be taken from elsewhere. For example, in a book review, proper attribution will indicate to a reader which quotes are from a book and which ones may be from an interview with the author.
- **Just ask for permission.** Many times, you can simply ask for permission to use certain excerpts of written work. There may even be larger parts that you'll be allowed to use that may be set aside for journalists.

  Here's how to find what you need:

  - Look for contact information via the author or publisher's website.
  - Request a media kit that may have more information on the work.

Photographs

Most types of stories and most mediums need them (even broadcast stories generally live online, where still photographs are necessary). But they're common sources of copyright infringement, causing up to $150,000 in damages *per photo.* Be extremely careful when it comes to using photos.

TIP

The general rules around using photographs are as follows:

- **Get permission from the person who took the photograph.** Make sure the person who's granting you permission actually took the photograph themselves. Otherwise, they don't legally have the authority to grant you permission to use it.

» **Get permission in writing.** When you get permission, don't just settle for verbal consent. Get it in writing. Some newsrooms even have a special form for such approval requests.

» **Be just as safe on social media.** You can easily let your guard down for images you want to post on social media, but social media images should also be posted with proper permissions. Unfortunately, there is no industry standard for this. Check with your newsroom for rules around social permissions.

Here's how to find what you need:

» Work with a photographer hired by your news organization.

» Take your own photos whenever you aren't able to work with a pro.

» Utilize photos with Creative Commons licenses that allow you to use them (see the nearby sidebar for more on Creative Commons).

» If you can afford it, pay for a news photo subscription or, for a more affordable option, pay per photo as needed. Wire services such as the Associated Press and Reuters allow you to do both.

CREATIVE COMMONS BASICS

Creative Commons is a nonprofit organization that is used to standardize the sharing of items such as photos, video, and audio. Colloquially, Creative Commons is the wide-ranging database of these items that is an essential resource for you as a journalist.

Here's what you need to know about Creative Commons:

- **You can find photos, videos, and audio.** Creative Commons is set up so that you can easily find and use items, so it can be your first stop when you need something for a story. For

(continued)

(continued)

example, instead of seeing if a photo has a Creative Commons license, search for Creative Commons works as your starting point. Use the Creative Commons site (`https://search.creativecommons.org`) as a tool to find what you need.

- **There are multiple licenses.** As a journalist, look for works that allow for commercial use. If you plan to edit the work in any way — for example, if you need to crop a photo — you also need to select a license that allows for adaptations. These are the two license selectors you should filter for during searches.
- **Stories are now being published using Creative Commons licenses.** In addition to items such as photos, more and more journalism organizations are expanding their reach by publishing full stories under Creative Commons licenses. This allows other journalism organizations to republish stories with proper attribution.

Videos

Getting video to use for stories is complicated because it's difficult to capture, and if you're seeking broadcast-quality video, it's even harder and more expensive to acquire. Rules around the permissions for video are similar to those for photos, but finding them may require a bit more work.

TIP

Here's how to find what you need:

- Similar to photos, recording your own video is best.
- Lean into user-generated video, by creating a process for finding, verifying, and getting permission for videos taken by news users. (This is common when needing video of weather events such as tornados, for example.)
- There are also video subscriptions and videos that you can purchase, but it's much more expensive to buy per asset. (For example, a photo on a newswire service can be about $35 for digital use, while a video from that same news event may be $500.)

Music and audio

Music isn't necessarily needed for many types of news stories, but if you're an audio journalist working on certain feature stories or podcasts, you'll likely need it.

Here are the rules around acquiring music:

- **Never ever just use commercial music.** All the music you hear on the radio is pretty much off-limits for journalism work.
- **Look for music that was made for content creators.** Music sites that make music specifically for people who make videos and podcasts often have affordable pricing. For example, try Epidemic Sound (`www.epidemicsound.com`).
- **Invest in your theme song.** If you want a special song for a podcast project that will be used over and over again, invest in purchasing a song you really like and then utilize free music for other sound design needs.

TIP

Here's how to find what you need:

- Search for free music and, if your project is not for commercial use, music that may be available for specific reasons.

  When I first started podcasting as a grad student, I found a musician who made music for educational purposes and allowed me and others to use it with attribution. There is a lot of music out there that you can take advantage of in the right and legal way.
- Talk with local musicians. They may want their music to be used with credit so that they can get some exposure.
- Look for music subscription services if you plan to do a lot of this work. It can be helpful to have a database you can search through easily.

Defamation/libel

People can argue that something posted about them in a journalism story is factually incorrect and that it *defames* them, or damages their reputation. The key to this argument is that the party is saying that what you published about them is untrue.

When journalists are accused of defamation, *libel* is the term that's used in court. Libel is defamation that is published in a physical form — in printed stories, in visuals or images, or online, for example.

TECHNICAL STUFF

The term for defamation that is spoken is *slander*, but *libel* is still usually used for TV and radio mediums. *Libel* would likely be used for broadcast defamatory statements that are seen as more permanent (for example, in a formal story and archived online), while *slander* may be used for a fleeting statement that someone says off-the-cuff during a show.

For a statement to be libel, it generally must be

- **Negligent, reckless, or intentional:** This metric shows that the journalist either intentionally tried to harm the person or didn't care if there would be harm.
- **Published:** If the defamation wasn't actually published, then it doesn't legally count.
- **Damaged someone's reputation:** There has to be measurable damage that can be shown and proven in court.

In these examples, the affected parties could likely attempt to sue for libel in a court of law:

- A blog spreading an unfounded rumor about a celebrity
- A newspaper accusing a company of wage theft without any proof and without reaching out to the company
- A broadcast TV segment showing an average person's face and saying they were accused of a crime, resulting in the loss of their job

TIP

Because libel has a very specific legal definition, a journalist must work within it. Here are some ways to defend yourself:

- **The truth:** Proving that what you published is, indeed, true is the ultimate way to fight libel claims.

- **Opinion:** If the statement was shared in an opinion piece as an opinion and not as fact, you can argue this defense.
- **Fair comment:** Similarly, if you're making a comment that criticizes something or someone (for example, art criticism), you can show there was no malicious intent.

Here are some examples for which it would be difficult to legally charge a journalist for libel:

- A story saying that a play was "unwatchable"
- A sports show talking poorly about a play on the field
- A story that exposes wrongdoing — of which you have proof

REMEMBER

Common, everyday citizens are afforded a level of privacy that high-profile people are not — and it makes sense. Famous people, people in government, celebrities, and other people who are in the spotlight can protect themselves and their reputations in a way that most people cannot. So, getting facts wrong about regular people can be extremely detrimental. Although public figures can and do sue for libel, they have a higher burden of proof — a higher level of harm that they must prove.

TIP

When you're trying to avoid defaming regular people, here are some areas to think about:

- Sharing the names of people accused of crimes who have not yet had their time in court and who do not pose a threat to the public
- Publishing mug shots and videos without blurring out faces
- Updating older stories that shared the names of people who were later deemed innocent

REMEMBER

Never publish a story accusing someone of doing anything negative without reaching out to them or their representative for comment. If they respond, publish their response in your story. If they don't respond, just say that in the story. But always give people the opportunity to explain themselves and respond to any wrongdoing.

Breach of contract

If you promise to keep the name of a confidential source anonymous, you can't publish their name without being in breach of contract. Ethically, you shouldn't make this promise to sources unless you're sure you can uphold it. Many courts see it as a binding agreement, similar to a verbal contract.

Contempt of court

On the other side of confidentiality, if a state doesn't have laws that protect journalists from keeping their confidential sources anonymous, a court may hold you in contempt for not sharing where or who you got your information from. Understanding the laws in your state is essential.

Plagiarism

Of course, as you learned at a young age in school, *plagiarism* (taking other people's work) is an ethical no-no. However, it can also be seen as a legal form of theft.

Sedition

WARNING

Although it's no longer a crime in the United States, publishing anything that criticizes the actions of the government can be seen as *sedition* (inciting a rebellion against the government). This act can be considered a crime that results in imprisonment in many countries, so it's important to understand this risk if you're working internationally.

Protecting Yourself as an Independent Journalist

Journalists who work in large newsrooms often are supported when dealing with legal issues because their employers either have in-house legal counsel or pay lawyers to be on retainer. Independent journalists, however, do not have that same luxury.

So, it's important to know what the laws are, how to protect yourself, and where to find help when you need it.

Looking into your state's reporter's shield laws

When discussing journalist's privilege, the laws that govern these in each state are called *shield laws.*

The Digital Media Law Project (www.dmlp.org) has created individual guides on shield laws per state. These guides explain

- **Who the laws protect:** Who is categorized as a journalist in your state and how
- **What information the laws protect:** Whether the identity of all sources or just sources who are promised confidentiality is protected and if it protects unpublished information
- **How strong the protections are:** Whether all information is protected or only pertinent information is protected

Journalist's privilege can be either absolute or qualified. *Absolute* means it applies to anyone who fits the definition of a journalist, while *qualified* privilege is conditional and only applies in certain situations. (Head to Chapter 11 for more information.)

Turning to the Reporters Committee for Freedom of the Press

Organizations that can provide legal assistance for journalists can fill in the gap for independent journalists who lack the institutional support of a newsroom. That's where the Reporters Committee for Freedom of the Press (RCFP; www.rcfp.org) comes in.

Here are some ways to utilize this helpful resource:

- **Pro bono legal representation:** If you get into a legal jam, you can reach out to the RCFP.

* **Amicus curiae support:** *Amicus curiae* means "friend of the court." When you share information to assist in a court case, the organization can help you.
* **Training:** Learn things like how to know when you need a lawyer and meet the organization's lawyers to ask them questions in their series of interactive trainings and workshops.
* **Guides:** When reporting on things like elections and the government, guides help you stay in step with legal limits.

To contact the RCFP for legal help, you can fill out an online form that is available to journalists Monday through Friday, 9 a.m. to 5 p.m. Eastern time. If you have an emergency outside of those hours (for example, you're arrested), you can call the Reporters Committee Legal Hotline directly at 800-336-4243. Before going out to cover a protest, write this number on your press badge and save it in your cell phone.

IN THIS CHAPTER

- » Understanding both the benefits and potential issues with new technological tools
- » Thinking through new ethical lines to draw as guiding boundaries

Chapter 13 Using Artificial Intelligence Tools

Artificial intelligence (AI) is everywhere online. It's integrated into almost every social media app, it's in most online software and tools you use daily (think Google Docs), and it's growing even more rapidly than most of us could've imagined decades ago.

TIP

AI has a wide-ranging definition, but it's helpful to think of it simply as computers doing tasks previously deemed "intelligent" — anything that involves reasoning, problem-solving, and analysis, for example.

But how and where does AI show up in journalism? The industry is still working to figure out its proper role. Even with much trepidation and resistance from journalists who don't want to embrace AI at all, it's still being used in many ways throughout journalism, in many mediums, and on many platforms. In newsrooms across the country, AI is automating tasks, replacing writing, and/or replicating production work.

Although the efficacy and ethics of using AI continue to be discussed, one thing is clear: AI's involvement as part of journalism innovation is not going anywhere. It's here to stay, and because of this likely long-term relationship, it's important for journalists to know just what AI can do and how to create ethical boundaries that align with the boundaries already established for the industry.

REMEMBER

When thinking through the ethics of AI, go back to the basics of the journalism ethical code (see Chapter 10):

- Truthfulness and accuracy
- Impartiality and fairness
- Independence and transparency

If you're evaluating whether using a tool in a certain way is ethical, think about these tenets and if anything could be crossing a line. For example, if using an AI-generated image would lead audiences to believe it's real when it's not, that would go against truthfulness and accuracy, so you would not use the AI tool in this way at this time.

In this chapter, I cover how the journalism industry is approaching AI, the potential it could hold for the future, and how you can best prepare for AI in the newsroom.

Looking toward the Future with AI

Much of the discussion around AI is not about what the technology is doing for journalism today, but what it can possibly do for it in the future. As I write this, in 2024, some newsrooms have started to experiment with AI, but not to the extent of what advocates of it say it can or will do. As with all new innovations, there are still many flaws in how AI is working.

But as AI evolves and works better and better, many people have high hopes for what it can eventually do for efficiency. Adopting these emerging technologies is often seen as a smart, pragmatic choice, especially as newsrooms balance mounting financial pressures with resource needs.

Here's a look at how supporters envision newsrooms as fully immersed, AI workplaces:

- **Helping in the creation of journalism:** Some people believe AI's role in making journalism is to automate as many small tasks as possible to free up journalists to do the heavy-lifting tasks they do best — things such as interviewing people and making tough decisions.

  WARNING

  Although some people identify the potential in automating tasks for journalists, many others worry about it opening up room to replace the work of some people in the newsroom completely. This fear is not unfounded, nor is it unrealistic. According to the Bureau of Labor Statistics, the number of people employed at newsrooms has continued to drop since the 2000s, and it is projected to decline slightly through 2032. The fear that decision-makers could see AI as a way to replace human labor completely, instead of as a tool to assist employees, is legitimate and real.

- **Helping in the distribution of journalism:** Today, we often talk about AI in regards to the journalism we make. But the opportunity of AI to assist in how it's shared with audiences is quite large. So much work goes into trying to understand audience trends and what the public wants. AI can help in this area.
- **Developing products for newsrooms:** In what is described as both a positive and a negative, companies that create AI tools may drive the production and innovation of the products that journalists use. Newsrooms won't have to worry about creating tools themselves, but these "platform companies" will have control over the products.

REMEMBER

These areas are already being explored today, which has led to researchers seeing the potential of what an expansive future with AI could be. But, as I write this, it's unclear how close we are to such a future. There are still significant issues with many AI tools and they need significant oversight when used.

Seeing How Newsrooms Are Currently Using AI

Even though AI isn't yet fully integrated into journalism, many journalism organizations are still experimenting with it. And for good reason: Newsrooms don't want to be left out.

As I mention earlier, AI is far from perfect. It isn't yet at a point where it can totally fulfill all its promises to transform the journalism industry. But for journalists who are open to trying new trends — especially those who are seeking immediate solutions to resource problems — the initiation of AI tools into the newsroom has been helpful. In fact, it has opened up the industry's eyes to how it may actually look in the future as the technology innovates.

In the following sections, I walk you through the various ways newsrooms are using AI in 2024 and the processes you can try.

Research and reporting

Generative AI is a type of AI that creates content. This type of content is often what the average person thinks of when they think of what an AI tool produces. Popular free tools such as ChatGPT (`https://chatgpt.com`) have become known for helping people do everything from writing summaries of books to brainstorming shopping lists.

Similarly, journalists have implemented similar large language models (LLMs) to help in the research and reporting process. These AI tools are being used to:

- **Find trends for story ideas.** Analyzing what audiences are talking about, as well as looking at what's being reported in other news media, is how journalists find stories that are meaningful and helpful for the public.
- **Brainstorm headlines.** Having the best headlines is extremely important in stories that are posted online because audiences determine if they'll click on a story to read it based on the headlines they read. AI can help

reporters think through certain keywords that may best appeal to audiences.

- **Transcribe interviews.** Transcribing interviews has historically been a large time sink for journalists because there was no real way to do it more quickly. AI drastically cuts the time it takes to transcribe an interview, and even if the transcription isn't perfect, it can help journalists quickly find the responses they need and edit them.

TIP

Some AI transcription tools are better than others. This is especially true when transcribing speakers who don't have the "perfect" *General American accent* (the accent used by reporters and anchors on national news broadcasts). Spend some time trying out these transcription tools, using free versions and free trials until you find one that's worth the investment.

Writing

After researching and reporting, journalists and journalism organizations are also using AI as part of the writing process.

WARNING

Using AI to write is one of the more controversial uses because it has the potential to be abused and, as I explain earlier, used to replace human labor.

When people think of AI writing, they may immediately envision college students using ChatGPT to write their term papers, but AI is being used in some creative ways to augment the work in newsrooms — without necessarily replacing the valuable work of journalists.

Here are some of the ways you may find AI working during the writing process:

- **Writing summaries for reporters' own stories:** If you view some of the websites of the largest news sites in the United States, you may notice AI summaries added to the tops of stories. These summaries are meant to better serve audiences seeking quick answers to the questions they're asking. It also helps those who prefer to read a summary instead of the full story.

TIP

Oftentimes, these AI summaries may note that they were written by AI but checked by a human to ensure they were accurate. This shows transparency to the audience and a commitment to accuracy. It's a way to embrace new technology while also ensuring the integrity of the overall story and journalistic ethics.

» **Writing stories in a template:** Some newsrooms may have stories that can be plugged into a template and that don't require interviews. Stories about game scores and company earnings reports are all written the same way and are based on numbers and math. Deeper stories about these same topics, though, would not work as an AI-written story.

» **Fact-checking stories:** Now more than ever, journalism organizations are implementing stories that fact-check speeches and conversations from events. In order to update these quickly, they utilize AI.

  But note that, as I write this in 2024, AI tools fall far behind in their ability to fact-check without the help of human intervention. They're known to sometimes make up information and even reference stories that don't exist. So, when newsrooms use them for fact-checking, they use tools created to source information only from certain places and as part of a process that involves people who double-check their results.

» **Editing copy:** AI can check drafts for grammatical errors and typos, as well as for style. Although using human editors is still the best way to look for issues in stories, many newsrooms can no longer afford to hire as many editors as they previously could. Some have lessened the number of checks and balances they had before, so AI is stepping in as one of those checks.

Creating audio and video

When creating audio and video stories, AI tools can help lessen the gap between beginner and intermediate producers and experts. Many AI tools are now already embedded within the editing software that journalists use, such as those within the Adobe Creative Suite.

Here are some ways you can use AI in your audio and video stories:

- **Cleaning up audio:** Sometimes, background sounds can distract from hearing the person being interviewed. AI tools can help remove — or lessen the sound of — the background noise.

  Some AI tools allow you to edit a person's quote so it sounds as if they said something they didn't. This is something a journalist would never do — it's just plain unethical. In the same way a journalist would never make up what a person says in a text story, they would never edit a person's quote to have them say something they didn't say. Never.

- **Creating video transcripts:** Video transcripts are extremely important so videos are accessible to everyone. But transcribing what everyone says and lining up each caption accurately can be extremely time-consuming. AI can do it quickly, and the reporter can just edit any captions that are incorrectly transcribed after.
- **Smoothing out bad cuts:** Sometimes, smoothing out rough video and audio cuts is really tough. AI tools are created to do it automatically.
- **Adjusting colors:** One goal of editing a journalism video is to adjust the colors in the video to match what they look like to the naked eye. That's why reporters and editors color-correct videos. AI can correct the color automatically.

Even if AI tools are within the same editing software journalists have used for years, it's important to still use them within the confines of what an expert would be able to do *without* the AI tool. For example, I work a lot in audio editing, and now there are AI tools that can change what a background sounds like in an interview. Because I can't make such drastic changes without AI, I wouldn't use it. That would be using AI unethically because it's not what I captured when I recorded the interview and it's not truly what that environment sounded like. This is not the same as maybe lowering background noise a bit to better hear the interview responses the same as I heard them in person.

I like to think about the shift to digital photography and what that meant for journalism. It meant that the edits you would make on a digital program like Adobe Photoshop would only be what you could make in an actual darkroom — adjusting the color, cropping, and fixing the tone — but not, say, removing something from a scene or removing a blemish from someone's face. The goal in that case is to get the picture to look how it looked in your eyes. Similarly, the goal with using AI in writing or with any other platform should be to stay within the confines of what truly happened and for you to best display that with editing.

Identifying Potential Issues to Look Out for with AI Tools

As helpful as AI can be, it can be equally problematic for journalists who use its tools to the full extent of their capabilities without thinking through those implications.

Inaccuracies and false sources

One of the largest problems journalists face when using AI tools is ensuring the accuracy of information during the news-gathering process.

Journalists using AI tools must ensure that:

- **The facts are correct.** Simply put, many of the facts AI tools gather may be incorrect. Here, you should go back to old-school reporting practices and verify everything.

REMEMBER

  Remember that old-school journalism adage, "If your mother says she loves you, find a second source." Even the smallest, most believable facts should still be fact-checked.

- **The sources are real.** Because it has become even easier to produce fake information with AI, many AI tools can pull from those false sources when scouring the internet for answers. Make sure these sources are real — and that they actually exist.

- **Any analysis is not misinterpreted.** LLMs are very smart in how they interpret what they read, but they can and do often interpret information incorrectly. For example, they may produce an interpretation of a reading that is the exact *opposite* of what the author intended. So, it's essential to double-check anything you get from AI.

Plagiarism

Plagiarism is a no-no in any sense, in any industry, and in any form. But it's important to note that AI makes it easier for people — especially writers — to plagiarize. It may even cause you to plagiarize on accident.

WARNING

Even if AI makes it easy to do so, here are some things you should never do:

- **Never make up sources with AI.** Journalists never, ever make up sources. This ethics rule continues regardless of technology.
- **Never make up quotes with AI.** Journalists never make up quotes. Only use what people have said. However, because the popularity of AI tools has grown, particularly LLMs or generative AI tools, some people have started to create stories based on what people *might* have said in an interview.

  For example, there have been stories about what historical figures might have thought about recent social issues. Not only is this unfair to those figures and their legacy, but it can become quite confusing if these "interviews" were to be accidentally taken as fact in the future. It's the complete opposite of your goal as a journalist, which is to tell the truth and be accurate.
- **Never let AI write for you.** You're a journalist — you do your own writing. Even if it seems as if you're working with an AI tool to write, it's still plagiarism to allow the AI to write any part of your work for you. (If you're a student in a journalism program, it's likely a violation of your academic code and could lead to an automatic expulsion from your program.)

Intellectual property

Many AI tools become smarter and smarter by learning from their input. But this means they're often building on and then repeating information that may be proprietary and should not be shared.

Here are two ways these tools may be infringing on intellectual property:

- **Giving you someone else's intellectual property:** You know never to let AI write your stories for you. But it's important to keep in mind that if you use AI to write something in your own files or notes, those words could have been pulled from another user's intellectual property.
- **Taking *your* intellectual property:** Anything you input into certain LLMs, such as ChatGPT, can become public. So, if you're working on an investigation or something else that is private and secretive, never add any of your work to this type of tool.

REMEMBER

Staying on top of how AI technology works is how you should focus on your goal to stay within the ethical boundaries of journalism. You don't want to extend those boundaries — just work on realizing how AI fits within them.

4
Using Different Media Platforms

IN THIS PART . . .

Delve into the many mediums of journalism.

Think through structural considerations and needed skills for various platforms.

Outline the roles and responsibilities of journalists working in different kinds of newsrooms.

Ponder working on the margins of journalism and the opportunities those roles present.

IN THIS CHAPTER

- » Understanding how print and digital organizations work
- » Looking at the differences between digital and print
- » Becoming a stronger print-style journalist
- » Knowing the roles of print and digital journalists in newsrooms

Chapter 14
Print and Digital

When people think of journalists, they often think about print media — the newspaper delivered by the neighborhood kid with a paper route. These days, however, many journalists write for digital outlets — online-only news sites (like `www.propublica.org` or `www.vox.com`), the websites of major TV networks (like `www.cnn.com` or `www.msnbc.com`), or newsletters (like `https://manchestermill.co.uk`, a Substack newsletter with local news about the Greater Manchester area in the UK).

In this chapter, I explain what you need to know to work in print journalism. I also talk about the different types of jobs you can have in print and what you can do to be successful.

Working in Print: The First Form of Journalism

The written word is the first form of recorded journalism. There was a news sheet in Ancient Rome called the *Acta Diurna* that was published every day. Historians say it published helpful info like events and public speeches, as well as what people wanted to know — things like gossip, births, and deaths. So, it's no wonder that newspapers, even with the significant changes they've sustained, remain one of the foundations of journalism today.

In addition to newspapers, print also includes magazines. Although they may not date back to Ancient Rome, the first magazine appeared in the 1600s and had more literary and philosophical content. This relates to how we often see magazines (including online or digital magazines) today. They're often places where writers can publish longer pieces; they're also often more relaxed in their writing and explore topics that may not easily find a home in a newspaper.

Some of the most popular types of magazines include:

- Beauty and fashion
- Sports and entertainment
- Health
- Business
- Travel and food
- Home lifestyle

These types of magazines all fit within the category of consumer magazines because they're created to be bought and read by audiences directly.

TIP

Outside of consumer magazines, there are also other types of magazines that can help new journalists get magazine writing experience:

- **Trade magazines** are made for specific industries and those who work in them — for example, *Popular Mechanics, Packaging World,* and *Publishers Weekly* are for those in the mechanics, packaging, and publishing industries, respectively.
- **Company magazines** are written as part of a company's editorial work — for example, the magazines you read on planes that are created by the airlines themselves.

PRINT: THE FOUNDATION OF JOURNALISM

In traditional journalism programs in colleges and universities, it's common for students to take introductory classes that have evolved from newspaper-specific courses. Even if students plan to go into other fields as their primary medium for reporting, knowing how to write and report for a newspaper is seen as a fundamental skill. In such courses, topics include:

- **News judgment:** What stories are chosen to be in a newspaper
- **Newswriting:** How you write for a newspaper and traditional newspaper story structures
- **News reporting:** How you report stories that fall within the normal newspaper beats

Seeing How Digital Differs from Print

When stories are online, there are additional considerations that journalists must make. So, for many people, even the same stories that are present in a media organization's print publication may be different online in the following ways:

» **It may have a different headline.** When a headline is written for print, it often focuses on space (not being too long) and being catchy. For example, think of the eye-catching headlines you may find on a newspaper's front page. But when those same stories are published online, editors must consider what headlines will make the most sense when they're viewed on the website and on social media.

They also have to think about what words people will be searching for to find the story. Purposely including words that are heavily searched for is called *search engine optimization* (SEO).

» **It may use different and/or more photos.** Due to space and layout constraints, a print story can't use as many photos as an online story can. Digital stories also can include slideshows and videos. The main photo may be different online if it doesn't look good when shared on social media.

» **It may be longer.** Many stories have to be cropped for print, not because it's the best length for the story but because it has to fit the allotted space. A longer version of the story can live online without those cuts.

» **It may include sidebars.** Sidebars can help share relevant information. Posting a story online gives you the opportunity to add multiple sidebars to include information that may not fit within the regular story but that your audience may still want to read.

TIP

Many of the decisions that are made about print stories traditionally stem from limits that are just inherent to that medium. Publishing a story online removes many of those constraints. The shift in mindset is to prioritize the audience instead of any strict rules that were created for those print reasons. When you're publishing online, think about what makes the story easier to find, scroll through, and digest.

Identifying the Traits of Top Print and Digital Journalists

Print and digital journalists have unique skills that make them great at their jobs. They know how to write, yes. But it takes more than just having an innate talent that makes you good at *this* type of writing. Journalism writing is very specific, with many things that vary from the writing you may do every day — even if you write a lot for work in a corporate or academic setting.

The goal for any journalist is to figure out the best way to get information to audiences. So, you need to approach the process differently and focus on different skills.

Here are just some of the things print and digital journalists master in order to do their jobs:

- **Grammar and punctuation:** The most important part of writing is having a strong grasp of grammar and punctuation. Things like ensuring that subjects and verbs agree in our writing are part of foundational writing knowledge and allow you to have a strong base for building journalism-specific skills.

  WARNING

  If you use any artificial intelligence (AI) tools to help you improve your grammar and punctuation by fixing mistakes, make sure you don't allow it to rewrite your sentences for you. This is essentially a form of plagiarism because it's no longer using your own words.

- **Writing concisely:** Journalism writing is specific in nature and different from other kinds of writing — academic writing, for example — because the goal is to get straight to the point. You use words efficiently and avoid flowery language and extra words that aren't needed. This focus helps you get your point across to audiences and clearly convey information.
- **Writing quickly:** In addition to writing concisely, writing quickly is a specific and essential skill for any journalist. When breaking news happens, it's often an "all hands on deck" situation in many newsrooms, so you'll often have to write breaking news stories, even if it's not the main thing you do. Also, in daily news, it's important to get stories written, edited, and published within a few hours of the news occurring — even if it's not urgent or considered "breaking."
- **Outlining:** Strong news writers are good at outlining because they understand that story structure is key to getting information out efficiently. With the most important and relevant facts at the top of the story, print-style stories

are written differently than you may write an essay or college paper, for example. So, it requires thinking about what information goes where.

REMEMBER

Outlining may feel unnecessary, but it definitely is the key to synthesizing what you've learned and transferring it into a story draft.

- **Basic photography:** Words need images — they pull readers in and get them interested in what you've written. So, it's important for journalists to have basic photography skills, even if they're primarily writers. As newsrooms continue to tighten their budgets, it's even more important for all journalists to know how to take photos for their own stories and not rely on others to provide photos for them. Plus, in most cases, the photos you take are likely better than any stock images or generic photos your newsroom may have on hand to use.

TIP

You can take amazing photos for your stories with your smartphone. Get in the habit of practicing taking multiple photos with different orientations to help with different layout needs for print and the various cropping needs for digital.

- **A knowledge of Associated Press (AP) style:** Although every media organization eventually creates its own style for its newsroom, the *Associated Press Stylebook* is most often the foundation for many of these guides. It's adopted internationally and is the most widely used style guide around. Because of this, journalists are expected to have a strong grasp of common AP style.

TIP

The *AP Stylebook* is available as an actual book, as well as an online, searchable version. One very helpful tool that assisted me when I was first learning AP style was its study guides, which I bought as an add-on to my online subscription. They included quizzes that helped me really figure out what I didn't know and what I didn't understand. So much of AP style was confusing to me at first, so investing in and using this tool was worth the time and extra effort.

TAKING CLASSES OR WORKSHOPS TO IMPROVE YOUR PRINT JOURNALISM SKILLS

Print journalism skills are ever-evolving. So, we all should work to continue to improve them. Here are classes you can find without being enrolled in a journalism program that will improve your skills:

- **Interviewing:** Interviews are essential to your reporting and having enough information to mold into a good story. Working on your interview skills can help improve how you ask questions and your confidence in these environments.
- **Editing:** There are many courses available to journalists who want to be better at editing stories. They can be helpful if you'd like to be an editor one day, but these classes also help you learn how to better edit your own work and work better with your own editors.
- **Photography with a DSLR camera:** Knowing how to use a digital single-lens reflex (DSLR) camera is helpful. If no one in the newsroom is available to teach you, a class can help.
- **SEO optimization:** Because even print organizations are — or soon will be — worrying about SEO, learning more about it will put you ahead of the curve in many media organizations.

LinkedIn Learning (`www.linkedin.com/learning`) has many free courses that are related to journalism that are often provided free through some companies and universities. If you don't have access to a free subscription, there is also an inexpensive subscription option that allows you to take multiple courses and get certifications and badges that are visible on your LinkedIn profile.

Writing in Print Style

Print stories should flow in a specific way. When you're writing in this style, here are some important things to keep in mind:

» **Think about how you're answering the *who, what, when, where, why,* and *how* of the story.** Above all, providing the necessary facts that readers need to know is essential.

For example, if you're doing a story about a fire that just occurred, you may not yet know how it started or why, but when you think through what your readers would want to know immediately, you can likely answer:

- What happened
- Where it took place
- Who, if anyone, was hurt
- When the fire started
- When it was put out

» **Avoid any repetition, including interviewees who say very similar things.** To save space and to be as concise as possible, print-style writing doesn't often repeat things. Cut similar quotes or cut out interviewees to leave space for those who have varying responses. You should also avoid saying the same words multiple times.

For example, after saying Walmart once, other references may be to the "retail giant" or the "Arkansas-based retailer" to avoid saying the name over and over.

» **Focus heavily on headlines.** *Headlines* (sometimes referred to as *titles*) are essential because they're the first thing that audiences read. Headlines are just as important to a story as anything else. Although editors often write or modify headlines, it's a skill that's important for everyone to have. Reporters who can write headlines are an asset to a newsroom.

TIP

The subhead that comes accompanies the headline is often called the *dek* or *deck*. In drafts, you'll often see this written as follows:

- Hed:
- Dek:

In the following sections, I give a primer on print style writing and explain the basis for approaching such stories.

Following the inverted pyramid

You can't take an introductory journalism course without talking about the inverted pyramid. And that's because, for years and years, it has been the standard for how most print news stories have been written.

The inverted pyramid structure came to be for a very pragmatic reason: so that when people were manually typesetting stories to be printed in the newspaper, the least important details were on the very bottom of the story and could easily be cut for space.

In today's electronic world, where print layouts are made on computers, you'd think there'd be no reason for this structure. But it has proven to be a very effective way to share information.

Here's how the inverted pyramid (shown in Figure 14-1) works:

- **The top:** The top of the pyramid is where the most essential information in a story lies.
- **The middle:** The middle of the story has a lot of important details that add to the top.
- **The tail:** The tail has the smaller, less important miscellaneous details — details that could be cut without losing any meaning in the story.

Here's exactly what could be in that top portion:

- **The lead:** A standard news lead, sometimes spelled *lede,* is a one-sentence paragraph that includes as much of the *who, what, when, where, why,* and *how* of the story that I mention earlier. When you're writing the lead, you want to be extremely clear. You also want to think about whether:
  - Any people of prominence should be mentioned by name
  - Any background facts that can't wait for the next paragraph should be provided
  - Anything should be summarized and included

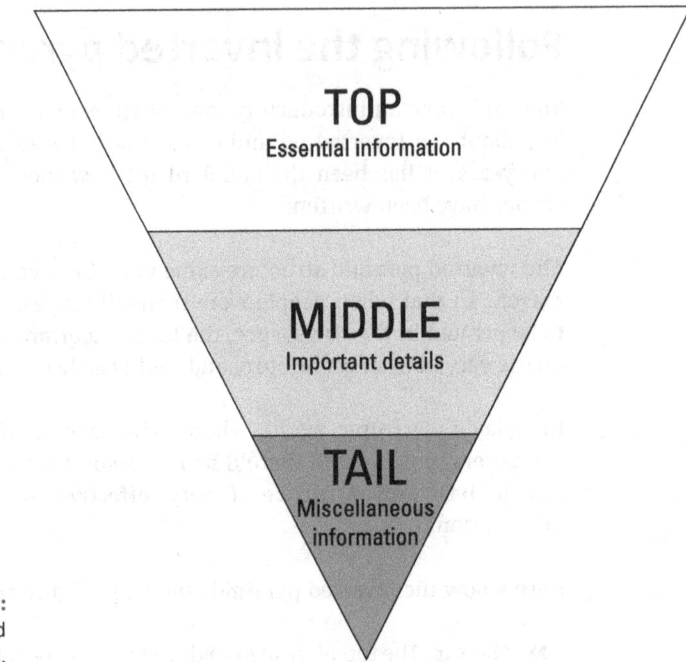

FIGURE 14-1: The inverted pyramid.

© *John Wiley & Sons, Inc.*

TIP

A standard lead is not the only kind of lead. But it's the most common for many stories.

- **A more descriptive paragraph:** After the lead, there is usually a paragraph that adds more of the essential details to the story. It usually includes what couldn't fit in that first paragraph, because the lead should be a single sentence.
- **A strong quote:** A good quote may also be at the top of the story.

TIP

When choosing quotes, avoid using any quotes that just give information — those kinds of should be paraphrased for conciseness. Look for quotes that show emotion; have specific, strong language; and translate well in print.

- **The nut graph:** The *nut graph,* sometimes spelled *nut graf,* explains the nut or the kernel of the story. It's where you explicitly explain to the reader why this story is important. You can do this by:

* Including statistics about how many people are affected by something
* Adding a time element that shows the story is relevant *now*
* Help the reader consider how an issue — or solution — is affecting people

REMEMBER

Every written story should have a nut graph. Don't forget about this very important part.

Writing features and profiles

Feature and profile highlight the uniqueness of a person, place, group, or organization. The goal with these stories is to do so by showing an up-close-and-personal look at them.

Features and profiles generally follow the rules of other print stories, but they have some unique differences that help them flow and read smoothly.

Here are some things you'll find in a feature story or profile of a person:

» **They often have an anecdotal lead.** An anecdotal lead tells a story. That story has description, details, and quotes. It can be used for a story in which there is a person who is affected by an issue or is part of a new solution. For example, if you're writing a story about a program that helps people pay their property taxes, a story about a person who used the program would work for an anecdotal lead.

» **They may not follow the inverted pyramid.** These stories may take elements from the inverted pyramid structure, but they generally don't follow it. They still have a nut graph, though, because they should show the reader why the story is so important.

TIP

Even when you aren't writing using the inverted pyramid, the nut graph should still be rather close to the top of the story, maybe within the first third — depending on its length — because you don't want to wait too long to explain to readers why they should care about the story.

» **They likely have more detail-oriented storytelling.** Although you still write concisely and clearly, features and profiles leave room for more tiny details, such as what people wear, how places look, and more.

REMEMBER

Many of the differences that you'll find in features and profiles are natural to implement when you think about their purpose and what would be best for the reader. Remember to always keep your audience in mind when you write. Ask yourself, "Is what I'm writing best expressing this story to the audience?"

Using style guides

Style guides are really important to help create order in how things look and feel. The *AP Stylebook* is the most popular guide for newsrooms. Because of its popularity, it's important for journalists to have a strong grasp of AP style.

But there are AP style entries for hundreds of pages of things. There's no way that you can learn everything. You can, though, memorize the style for things you write over and over again every day, and you can learn what you should always look up.

Top entries to look up in the *AP Stylebook* include:

» **Numbers:** In AP style, you spell out numbers under ten and then use numbers for everything that is ten and above. But you should still look up this rule, because there are certain cases where it doesn't apply. For ages of people, measurements, temperatures, and speeds, for example, you always use numerals.

TECHNICAL STUFF

Don't look to this book for examples of AP style. This book was edited mostly in line with the *Chicago Manual of Style*, as well as the style guide unique to the *For Dummies* series. The *Chicago Manual of Style* is commonly used in book publishing.

» **Capitalization:** Capitalization is one of the trickier things to get a grasp on in AP style. It's one to double-check often.

» **Addresses:** Addresses are specific in AP style because certain kinds of streets are abbreviated as part of an address (street, avenue, boulevard), but others are not (circle, road, parkway).

- **Cities and states:** In the body of a story, AP style dictates that you never abbreviate states. But you do abbreviate them when a state is part of a *dateline* (the line at the beginning of the story that shows where the story was reported). However, some major cities don't need a state when they're used in a dateline so the state is not included at all.
- **Titles:** Most of the time, titles are only capitalized when they're used as part of a proper noun in front of someone's name. But this is only true for certain titles, such as president, not other titles, such as professor. Most titles are not abbreviated, but some military titles are.
- **Dates:** Some months are abbreviated when they're part of a full date. But when those months are not part of a full date, they should be spelled out. For example, in AP style, you would say "Jan. 1, 2026," but "January 2026."

TIP

For special events and happenings, like the Olympics for example, the *AP Stylebook* creates special guides that accompany the stylebook and sends them out to everyone who is subscribed to it and to its alerts. This specific guide has information compiled in an easy way that helps you more easily find what you need to write about such events.

These seem like very small rules, but they help create uniformity and ensure that everyone in a news organization is writing — and editing — in the same way.

The *AP Stylebook* alone doesn't cover everything. In fact, it historically has been slow to update its guidance to be in alignment with societal changes. For example, it was not quick to incorporate gender-neutral language. This has led many other reputable groups to create their own style guides.

TIP

The following guides, many from journalism advocacy organizations, can be extremely helpful:

- **The Asian American Journalists Association Style Guide:** `www.aajastyleguide.org`

» **Guía Antirracista for Spanish-Language Newsrooms (by the Craig Newmark Graduate School of Journalism's Center for Community Media):** `www.journalism.cuny.edu/2021/06/guia-antirracista-for-spanish-language-newsrooms`

» **The National Association of Black Journalists (NABJ) Style Guide:** `https://nabjonline.org/news-media-center/styleguide`

» **The National Association of Hispanic Journalists (NAHJ) Cultural Competence Guide:** `https://nahj.org/wp-content/uploads/2020/08/NAHJ-Cultural-Competence-Handbook.pdf`

» **NLGJA: The Association of LGBTQ+ Journalists Stylebook:** `www.nlgja.org/stylebook-on-lgbtq-terminology`

» **The Trans Journalists Association Stylebook and Coverage Guide:** `https://styleguide.transjournalists.org`

» **The Tribal Nations Media Guide (by the Native American Journalists Association):** `https://indigenousjournalists.org/wp-content/uploads/2020/10/2020-NAJA-Tribal-Nations-Media-Guide-1.pdf`

A group of journalists got together to create a guide called Language, Please (`https://languageplease.org`). Not only is this site free, but it's being consistently updated with guidance on topics that are related to social, cultural, and identity issues. It's a great stop when you need to figure out how to write about a tough subject.

HOW STYLE GUIDES CAN GUIDE MORE THAN THE WRITTEN WORD

When you think of style guides, you probably think of them guiding things such as capitalization and abbreviations. And it's true that they do help with uniformity. But way more important than that is how style guides help people think through changes in society — and ways journalism can be more inclusive to everyone.

Many of the newer style guides, especially those created by journalism advocacy organizations, were created because there was a need to better report on issues facing different underrepresented groups. Because these guides exist, you have extra support in ensuring that you talk about everyone in a way that respects their identity, their cultural heritage, and who they are as people.

Everyone comes to journalism with their individual experiences, biases, and blind spots. You can't possibly know everything about everyone. But you should want to learn about everything and be committed to reporting on everyone in the best way possible.

Here are some instances in which you can turn to style guides to help you think through how to best do it:

- **When you're reporting on culturally relevant history:** Historical context is important in understanding history, so refer to guides when writing about historical events that may be associated with a certain group. For example, as NLGJA: The Association of LGBTQ+ Journalists explains in its stylebook, the coverage of HIV/AIDS has been intertwined with the coverage of LGBTQ+ people since the 1980s so it's included in its guide.
- **When you're reporting on a cultural event or celebration:** Whenever you're reporting on an event, take a moment to double-check the appropriate style guide to ensure you're discussing it correctly. For example, the Asian American Journalists Association Style Guide has an entry for Lunar New Year and explains to use a community's preferred celebration name when you're talking about it (for example, Chinese New Year or Spring Festival in China, Tet in Vietnam, and Seollal in South Korea).
- **When you're reporting on someone's identity:** Identity is complicated, for many reasons. So, in addition to always asking people how they choose to identify themselves, refer to guides for a better understanding. For example, the NAHJ Cultural Competence Guide has an entry discussing the difference between *Hispanic* and *Latino* and how the terms are not interchangeable.

Looking at the Roles and Responsibilities in Print and Digital Journalism

Newsrooms that are print- and digital-first are set up to prioritize the creation and publication of written stories. Although the structure may vary, most journalists primarily fall within the following three categories:

- People who write
- People who edit
- People who run the website

This is because writing good journalism stories is difficult, and it takes a team of people working together to consistently churn out stories.

In the following sections, I describe the job titles and responsibilities you're likely to find in a print newsroom.

People who write

TIP

If the product being published is actually something like a newsletter, that person may be called a writer instead of a reporter. The job of newsletter writer has grown in popularity as more and more people have started to use them as one of their primary means of getting news. Some newsletter writers do their own original reporting, while others may just do aggregate writing. Some also can do a mix.

REMEMBER

Aggregation is the practice of pulling from other journalists' reported stories to create your own instead of talking to sources directly.

Here's what the role of reporter may involve at a place like a newspaper or magazine:

- **Pitching stories:** Reporters stay on top of what's happening within their *beat* (subject area) and pitch stories related to them to their editor. Although stories they didn't pitch will likely also be assigned to them, they're responsible for coming up with their own ideas.

- **Getting out and interviewing people:** Most reporters will tell you that covering their beat requires them to go to events and be out and about. It's very difficult to find stories to write if you stay in the office behind a computer. Being a reporter requires you to go outside, leave the office, get in on the action, and see what's happening for yourself.

REMEMBER

The difference between reporting and simply doing research is this act of getting out from behind a screen. Reporting pushes you to physically be in the places you're going to be talking about in your story so you can experience them.

- **Writing stories:** Reporters are ultimately responsible for writing stories. This means that even with the assistance of editors and others in the newsroom, every single thing you write is yours, and readers will see it as such.

REMEMBER

Because it's your name on the byline of a story, you're still responsible for any mistakes that are in the story. Never leave it up to someone else to do a final read and fact-check of your work.

People who edit

As their name indicates, editors are in the formal position of being responsible for editing print and digital stories in these newsrooms.

REMEMBER

A newsroom can have different levels of editors who may do different things. So, it's possible to have higher-up editors who guide the newsroom's overall editorial mission but who don't actually edit individual stories. This is often the case in midsize and larger newsrooms.

Especially in the magazine industry, newer editors can join the ranks of editors in roles such as assistant editor and work their way up. Because editing is such a specific skill that people should be trained to do, there can be several sublevels even within the same area. For example, it's not uncommon for a magazine to have an assistant editor, an associate editor, and an editor all under its fashion vertical. (*Verticals* are a magazine's major subject areas or categories.)

Here are some skills all editors have in common:

» **Great news judgment:** One of the hardest things in journalism is figuring out how to go from an idea to a story. Great editors help reporters hone their story ideas into refined pitches. This is especially helpful when working with newer reporters who are still learning this skill.

REMEMBER

Every interesting issue or topic area isn't a story. It could possibly be a story, though, after it's polished into a specific angle.

» **Attention to detail:** How many editors touch a story before it's published varies by newsroom. So, it's important that editors have an extremely good eye. Sometimes a publication will have editors who do the big edits (edits for content) and other editors who do copyediting (for things like grammar, typos, and AP style). But many newsrooms have downsized their editorial operations, and it may be necessary for a single editor to catch everything for a story.

» **Communication skills:** It's not easy to give people feedback on what they need to improve. But editors should not only be giving reporters such feedback on their current stories, but also be expressing how they should do certain things better in the future. This requires a high level of communication that ensures that reporters can receive this information and retain it.

WARNING

It's a misconception that someone can be a great editor because they're a great reporter. Editing requires the ability to not only give feedback to reporters on their work, but also give those suggestions in a certain way. The best editors are also mentors of younger reporters, can encourage growth, and know how to pull out the best in people. So, if your aspiration is to be an editor, look specifically for editing trainings and workshops. Organizations such as the American Society of News Editors (`https://members.newsleaders.org`) offer trainings for new and aspiring editors.

People who run the website

Decades ago, media organizations wouldn't have dedicated staffers to run their websites. Anyone in the newsroom who was available — and capable — might've uploaded stories. But as newsrooms have embraced the benefits of an online presence and shifted to prioritizing their digital presence, it has become common to have teams of people who run the website.

The position titles of these roles vary greatly, as does how the responsibilities are divided. For example, all the tasks of running the website could fall to the same person, or they could be divided among different people, with each person focusing on doing one particular task really well.

However, all the tasks generally fall within these categories:

- **Publishing new stories:** Getting new stories up and onto the website must be done quickly and efficiently. This often includes doing an extra read of the text, choosing photos if there aren't any, and possibly writing or editing captions.
- **Monitoring the home page:** As news changes throughout the day, it's customary to swap out stories on a media organization's home page so readers see something new every time they visit. Some large news organizations have tools that can help them see what stories are being read the most to help them with this decision.
- **Posting and engaging on social media:** Although social media isn't technically part of a newsroom's website, posting on social media generally falls to this group of people. They also usually monitor how many people click on story links from these various posts and come to the website from them.

TIP

If you're savvy and you have strong digital skills, these types of roles may be a good way to get a foot in the door of a newsroom you really want to work at.

IN THIS CHAPTER

» Understanding what it's like to work in TV news

» Exploring different types of video storytelling in journalism

» Knowing the roles of journalists in video newsrooms

Chapter 15
Television and Documentary Video

When breaking news is happening, it's second nature for many Americans to pick up their remotes and turn on TV news. That's because, since the 1940s, television has been one of the main forms of giving the public essential information.

There are many reasons for television's popularity as a journalism media:

- It's easy to access.
- Video as a medium is compelling.
- You can see news unfolding live.

» Segments are often short and easy to take in.

» You can see what's happening for yourself.

TIP

People like TV because there is something special about being able to visually see what journalists are talking about. Often, seeing really is believing, and audiences often have a greater trust when they can literally see the news that is happening around them and around the world.

In this chapter, I explain what you need to know to work in video journalism. I also talk about the different types of jobs you can have in video and what makes video stories successful.

Seeing Where Video Journalists May Work

Although journalists who are trained to work in TV news generally do work in that field, that's not the only place they can use those skills. Video journalists could work at places like:

» National commercial networks (such as NBC, ABC, CBS, CNN, MSNBC, and Fox News)

» Local news affiliate networks

» Noncommercial networks, such as a PBS member stations

» Online-only news stations

» Documentary companies

» Digital publications with video reporting

The increase in job opportunities due to digital publications' growth has helped give video journalists more and more opportunities to explore their work. Of course, many journalists love working in TV, and it's their goal to always do so. But working in TV news, specifically, employment looks different from the way it does in other mediums of journalism.

DECIPHERING A TV NEWS EMPLOYMENT CONTRACT

Unlike other news organizations that hire employees at will, broadcast TV news organizations hire their employees under contract, often for periods of two to three years. These contracts are quite restrictive, so it's important to understand the commonplace terms you may see. Here's what you'll likely find in a contract that you may not have encountered in other types of employment:

- **An open list of services:** Even if you're hired for a specific role, your job can often reassign you as needed. So, such language is included in the contract.
- **Morals clause:** Especially if you're on-air talent, people will view you and your name as being synonymous with the news station. If you do anything that the station says is immoral or puts it in a bad light, you can be fired.
- **Noncompete clause:** Noncompete clauses are common in many industries, but they look quite different in TV news. Your contract may say that even after your contract has ended, you can't work for any TV newsroom your employer sees as a competitor. This may include all local newsrooms in your city, as well as those in nearby cities. The way this clause is phrased can force TV news journalists to move quite often.
- **Termination penalties:** As in other jobs, if your employer fires you before your contract is up, your contract generally details some kind of severance pay and package. This part of the contract is pretty standard. But what's different is what happens if *you* decide to leave the station before the end of your contract. If you terminate your contract early, you may have to pay the station money and you could also be sued.
- **Handling legal disputes:** If the newsroom determines that you're in breach of your contract and you want to fight it legally, your contract's choice of law clause says where and how that legal dispute must take place. For example, this clause may state that it has to happen in the state where you're working or it could be where the company is headquartered.

(continued)

(continued)

Contracts and the intricacies of how the TV news business works are why you should get an agent that specializes in TV talent. Many of these agencies exist for the sole purpose of representing you. They're well-equipped to help you negotiate your contracts. Some helpful things you might want to negotiate could be:

- What news stations count as competition
- Re-opening the contract for negotiations in certain instances, such as if you're reassigned to a different shift or duty
- Allowances for early terminations, such as if you get a job in a higher-paying market

Many TV news journalists who didn't have any representation when they negotiated their first job say they weren't equipped to handle the process. Some also say they agreed to terms that they didn't realize could be negotiated and then felt they had to stay at those roles, far past when they were ready to leave. So, it's worth it to get an agent or lawyer who can help you through the process and who has your best interest in mind.

Identifying the Traits of Strong Video Journalism Storytelling

Regardless of where video journalists work and whether they're on TV or a digital platform, their work has many key traits. Video is a strong mode of sharing information and telling stories, so even if a newsroom doesn't have a full video department, you'll likely find some form of video work in almost every newsroom.

Here are some of the things you'll see in strong journalism video storytelling:

- **Visuals are key.** With the "seeing is believing" mindset, stories must have a visual element. This means that journalists have to seek out multiple places to film and acquire different visuals in order to fully complete any video project.

TIP

When you watch documentaries, for example, think about how even the interviews are usually done in multiple settings and multiple angles. This ensures there is a collection of videos that look different and can add some variety to the look and feel of the story.

- **Time is short.** Outside of documentaries, which have a variety of lengths, most video stories are short. On TV news, a story may be as short as just 30 seconds. There is often a lot of information packed within a short time, which is quite hard to accomplish.
- **On-air personalities become part of the optics.** In stories that show a reporter, anchor, host, or any other kind of on-air journalist, those journalists are also personalities — people who are prominent and who become notable representations of their newsrooms or organizations.

  Within the actual story, on-air journalists become an essential part, being a guide for the viewer to get information, understand what's happening, follow an investigation, and so on.
- **The tone complements the brand.** The tone of the story should match the journalism organization's tone. So, not all video stories will cover a story the same way. For example, a TV newscast may take a straightforward approach in covering a missing person story, highlighting the facts only and keeping the tone informative, while a digital publication may want to do a feature that speaks more intimately with the missing person's family, has a tone that is more conversational, and includes more back and forth of the interview to lean into this.

Exploring Onscreen News and Long-Form Storytelling

Video storytelling can take many forms, but it's helpful to think of it in two ways:

- The shorter news stories you often see when you turn on your TV to watch the nightly news.

- The long-form stories that you often see as part of documentaries or 30-minute to hourlong shows (like *Dateline* or *60 Minutes*)

All these stories differ from print stories. One main difference is in how they're written. Writing scripts for videos requires writing in broadcast style. This often means switching up everything you may have learned in your other writing courses.

Basic broadcast writing rules include some important differences from print, including the following:

- **Sentence length:** Sentences in print are long, and you try to pack in as much information as possible. But that's not how people naturally talk. It's also difficult to take in all of that information without reading it. So, for broadcast writing, you rely on shorter sentences and make sure those sentences are easy to read on a script or teleprompter.
- **Attribution:** Attributing information or a quote to a source in print stories comes at the end of the sentence. But that's the exact opposite of how people speak naturally. In broadcast, you start all sentences with the attribution. For example, you say that "Authorities say" something happened.
- **Present tense:** In newspaper-style writing, everything has happened in the past. This rule has been standard in the industry for decades and decades. But the opposite is true for broadcast. In broadcast, you use present tense and active language to show how what you're discussing is currently unfolding. For example, when you say, "Authorities say," you're expressing that these are their current thoughts. When you say, "Police are investigating a crime," you're focusing on what's happening now and not the past crime.

This way of writing doesn't mean that you don't also give background information about what has already happened, but it does ensure that the language feels fresh and new. It also helps you highlight the most important and most updated piece of information in a story so it catches the ears of the audience.

» **Directness:** You should be direct in print stories, but there is more space to add in other details that may not be as essential. You don't have that space in TV. In broadcast stories, journalists use an easy-to-understand subject-verb-object structure that audiences can grasp quickly. There's no need for viewers to overthink these sentences because this structure is how people first learn sentences, and it's perfect for sharing information.

TIP

When you're writing your broadcast script, think of all the different things people do while they watch the news (for example, getting ready for work, cooking dinner, and handling parenting duties). Now, think about how you would talk to them knowing and understanding that you don't have their full attention.

When it comes to TV news, there are also many different types of shows. They have different structures, but they also work together to give audiences who watch a certain channel or network a wider variety of news stories. Here are some of the categories these shows may fall into:

» **Newscasts:** When you envision TV news, this is probably what you think about — a 30-minute or hourlong show with multiple short segments. It's what people mean when they say they're watching the six o'clock news, for example. Newscasts can also be multiple hours long, especially in the morning, to ensure people can catch up on information whenever they wake up.

» **Newsmagazines:** Newsmagazines cover current events, and they often have a mix of different types of segments that cover subjects like entertainment in addition to news.

» **Investigative newsmagazines:** Some of the most popular newsmagazines focus on investigative reporting. In them, they often cover a single story for the entirety of the program instead of having multiple segments.

» **Public affairs programs:** These programs are based on the news but also often have interviews, including panels and news roundups. Plus, they're often filled with commentary about news events that intend to further the information viewers received in other shows.

- **Talk shows:** Some talk shows feel more newsy and may fit in this category. This is especially true when journalists host such shows.

Identifying the Traits of Top Video and Documentary Journalists

Journalists who work in TV news and various video departments and those who work on documentaries may seem like they have completely different skill sets. But, actually, they likely have the same foundational training. That's because what makes a compelling video story is the same, whether it's for TV news or a documentary.

Here are just some of the proficiencies these journalists have:

- **Writing in a conversational way:** Writing in a way that feels natural when you read it is a specific skill. It shouldn't sound or look as if you're reading! So, in addition to using short sentences, present tense, and active language, journalists also write these sentences as if they're speaking.
- **Making every word count:** Whether it's a short news story or a long documentary, every word still counts in video. Journalists, along with editors and/or producers, strip unnecessary words and sentences from scripts to focus on emphasizing what's important.

TIP

Because every word counts, the longer the story, the more edits it will likely go through. Very short stories will only have time for a single edit before they air, while long documentaries will be edited for months or even years.

- **Thinking about B-roll:** As part of the story planning process, journalists think about all the different visuals that can help them tell the story. This is true even if they're working with a videographer. They still have a good idea about what video they may need before they even start filming.

B-roll is video footage that isn't the main action but can be used throughout the story to add to that main footage. For example, if you're reporting a story about a university's board of trustees' decision, you may have B-roll of random parts of campus, of students walking through the quad, or of signs that show the viewer exactly where you are.

TIP

Journalists can get creative when they lack enough main footage that they need for a story. That's why B-roll is so important. It can help fill in important gaps. Remember that video stories rely on visuals, and you can't do a story without strong imagery.

CLASSES OR WORKSHOPS TO IMPROVE YOUR VIDEO SKILLS

Video skills may be wide-ranging. But every single day, there are people taking video by storm without the help of traditional education. You can take classes in the following subjects without being enrolled in a journalism program in order to improve your skills:

- **Shooting and production:** Especially if you're shooting longer stories, learning how to do it takes some time and serious practice. Courses focused on using equipment, setting up your camera, making a shot list, and more can help you. One example is The Art of Visual Storytelling Specialization by the University of Colorado Boulder on Coursera (`www.coursera.org/specializations/the-art-of-visual-storytelling`).
- **Video editing:** One of the primary skills you need is editing video. Whether you think that'll be your responsibility or not, knowing how to edit your own video is essential. You can find courses on video editing everywhere. Some courses are even created specifically for people who work in TV news. One example is News Editing with Media Composer by Avid (`www.avid.com/courses/nc120-news-editing-media-composer`).

(continued)

(continued)

- **Interviewing:** If you plan to be an on-air journalist or even if you want to interview people in an off-screen role like that of a documentary producer, it's helpful to learn tips and tricks for interviewing. When you interview people who are on camera, you need to ask questions a certain way in order to get what you need on film. An example of a related course is Interviewing for TV & Film by BRIC Arts Media (`https://bricartsmedia.org/class/interviewing-for-tv-film`).

Making Great Video

Just as with writing, in journalism, there are rules around structure, length, and form when it comes to video. This guidance helps to ensure that video stories are made in a way that best helps audiences get the information they need.

Structuring a video story

Structuring video stories may differ from structuring a print story, but the process has some similarities. For example, in both print and video, short news stories require a much more simple structure and timeline, whereas longer, more feature-like stories allow you to explore more storytelling tools.

Of course, there are some key differences between video and print. Here are some of those distinctions you should know:

- **Split-page script:** Using a script that splits the page into two separate columns is something that is unique to video storytelling. Split-page scripts are formatted with:
  - A column on the left for video, which describes what will be shown on-screen
  - A column on the right for audio, which contains the journalist's narration (what's read aloud), as well as any other audio that's brought in such as music
  - Either a vertical line or just a well-spaced margin between the two columns

The visuals in the video column align horizontally on the page with the accompanying info in the audio column.

- **Catchy hooks:** Having a way to pull audiences in can look different depending on the subject of the story, but the goal is the same: to get viewers to stop and pay attention. You can do this by:
  - Teasing an interesting visual
  - Introducing a person with a relatable story
  - Asking a question
  - Giving surprising info
- **Strong endings:** Video stories should end just as strongly as they started — even the very short ones. Think about your ending as the final thing your viewers will hear from you and the thing that will leave a lasting impression. Some ways to end include:
  - Summaries
  - Creative zingers
  - Forward-looking info

TIP

If you're struggling to end your story, think about how you can be of service to the viewer. Ask yourself this: "If I were the viewer, what would I want to know?"

Looking at news package forms and lengths

You'll find multiple types of stories in a TV newscast, all slightly different but all with the purpose of giving viewers information quickly and in a short form.

REMEMBER

These stories are generally pretty short — often as short as 30 seconds.

They include:

- **Readers:** An anchor reads a story live for about 30 seconds.

» **Voiceovers (VOs):** An anchor's voice is heard over visuals for about 30 seconds.

» **Voiceovers to sound on tape (VOSOTs):** An anchor reads the first couple of lines of a story, and then a sound bite is played — all over visuals — for about 45 seconds or less.

» **Guest interview:** An anchor interviews a guest, Q&A style. The length varies.

» **Package:** A reporter prerecords and edits a story together with visuals. A package is often about one to two minutes but sometimes as long as three minutes.

Of these types, the news package is the story that TV journalists spend years perfecting. It's also the type of story that involves reporters going out in the field. Packages include:

» Narration

» Soundbites

» Video

» Natural sound

» Stand-ups

One thing people often visualize when thinking about TV news is a reporter doing a stand-up. A stand-up is when that person is standing in front of the camera talking directly into it. It can be for a planned, scripted package or it can be done live. Here are some things that journalists do during a stand-up:

» **Set up the story.** Talking to the camera to set up the story with important information is often helpful in ensuring the key information in a story is explained.

REMEMBER

If you're an on-air journalist, audience members likely see you as someone they know. So, when you're doing a stand-up, it can feel as if a person is explaining something to them in real life.

» **Wrap up the story.** Symmetry is important in many journalism story structures. So, ending a stand-up similar to how it started feels balanced. If you don't do this, it will feel as if you left the story and something will appear to be missing.

» **Show as much as they tell.** Remembering that these stories are short, a good journalist looks for nearby imagery to include in their visuals to add to the story. Extra points if there's something nearby that you can point to, pick up, or demonstrate in the story.

» **Show the action happening somewhere.** Although not all journalists who work with video work in front of the camera, it's likely that you either have to go live yourself or help an on-air journalist go live.

  Live stand-ups happen a lot in places such as sports or breaking news. It shows the audience what the environment is like and all the action happening around them.

  Some examples of this could be reporting:

  - Live from a basketball game where the crowd is loud and excited
  - Live from the scene of a fire where sirens are blaring everywhere
  - Live from a vigil where the mood is sad and somber
  - Live from a press conference where everyone is talking about a serious update that affects the city

TV journalists don't try to memorize every word. Many journalists just focus on sticking to an outline of points that they want to hit during a stand-up. Or if they do decide to memorize a script, it's for a very short stand-up (5 to 10 seconds at most).

REMEMBER

The goal is always to sound natural and not as if you're reading.

In addition to the stand-up, other important aspects of a package include:

» **An anchor intro:** This is what the anchor reads, usually from a teleprompter, before the package airs.

» **A clear structure:** Packages have a beginning, middle, and end that is easily seen. Some common parts include:

  - **The lead:** The first opening line that the reporter says

- **The open:** The first visual the viewer sees
- **The close:** The last line that the reporter says

» **A good mix of things:** It's important that a package isn't just you, the reporter, or just a sound bite, or just B-roll. A package is a well-edited story in which multiple elements play well together.

TIP

Always interview multiple people for your package. Even if most of those people don't make it into the final cut because of time, it's essential to understand various viewpoints and it's also key in getting quality quotes on tape.

Working on longer-form videos

Structuring shorter videos can be a lot of work, but at the end of the day, you're limited by time. Thinking through longer-form videos can be much more difficult because there is a lot of variety in how stories can be told when you remove the tight time constraint.

REMEMBER

When I use the term *long-form* in this chapter, I'm referring to stories that are documentaries or 30-minute to hourlong news shows.

For such videos, it may seem that there are fewer rules, but there are still many rules that can help guide your creativity. Newsmagazine shows, for example, are often in 30-minute or hour-long time blocks, and they have the same structure every day or every week.

There are even common structures for documentaries, which may not have the same exact constraints as news programs. But still, there are structural categories that help news people figure out how to start. Some documentary lengths include:

» **Shorts:** Documentary shorts are 5 to 30 minutes long.

» **Feature-length:** Between 75 and 120 minutes long, these documentaries run more like movies.

» **Docuseries:** Instead of trying to tell a story all at one time, docuseries break up the story into multiple episodes that are between 30 and 60 minutes each.

TIP

The story should determine the type and length of the long-form project. For example, you shouldn't choose a docuseries format just because you'd like more episodes. It should be because it's the best way to tell that story.

TIP

Starting your own long-form video project may feel intimidating. It's a lot of work to create something that long. But it doesn't have to be. There are some practices that you can learn to get comfortable with it. Here's some advice to get you started:

» **Try a three-act structure.** Draft your story into three acts to get started with structuring it. Think through how to plug it into the following parts, if possible:

- **First act:** The setup
- **Second act:** The conflict
- **Third act:** The climax

Think back to the types of stories you learned when you were first learning about rising action in elementary school. In those classes, the teacher broke down how the different parts of a story come together. This structure mirrors that idea.

» **Use storyboards.** *Storyboarding* is the practice of visualizing the story and its order by creating frames that represent what will happen in the video. It's part of the planning process that happens before you ever go and shoot anything, and its purpose is to:

- Help you think through your scenes.
- Brainstorm what the video could look like.
- Save you time and money.

» **Learn about observational versus participatory documentaries.** In observational documentaries, journalists are more removed from the story; in participatory documentaries, journalists are part of the story. For example, in participatory documentaries, you'll see the journalist interacting with interviewees and possibly traveling to uncover something in a participatory documentary, whereas in an observational documentary, the visuals and sound will do all the storytelling for you.

If you're wondering which route is best, here are some questions to consider:

- Will the story be more understandable and engaging if you help guide the audience?
- Will your presence in the story be a distraction?
- Will the story benefit from the journalist being seen and forming a personal connection with the audience?

Identifying the Roles and Responsibilities of a Video Journalist

Many, many people work in TV newsrooms. And similarly, depending on the organization, there could be just as many varying positions at documentary filmmaking companies and other journalism organizations that create video content.

WARNING

Although many journalists make documentaries, it's important to remember that not every documentarian is a journalist. So, their companies don't uphold journalistic standards in their work. As a journalist, it's important to work for companies that allow you to follow the journalism code of ethics.

Although there are many video journalism jobs, most of these roles fall within the following three categories:

- People who are on camera
- People who are behind the camera
- People who run the website

Making videos is hard work. Collectively, these journalists work together to ensure they adequately tell the stories they're supposed to tell.

In the following sections, I guide you through the job titles and responsibilities you may find in a video-first newsroom.

People who are on camera

Reporters, anchors, and hosts appear on camera.

Here's what the role of reporter entails:

- **Finding, pitching, and reporting stories:** Just as they would in any medium, TV reporters are responsible for coming up with their own stories. They sometimes are general assignment reporters (Gas), or they may cover a specific beat.
- **Collaborating with videographers:** Most reporters go out with a videographer and work with them to think through stories, shots, and more.

TIP

Although this does not apply to all reporters, it's now common for new reporters to be hired as multimedia journalists (MMJs) in TV newsrooms. Reporters who are MMJs must shoot and edit their own packages so they don't have videographers out in the field with them. It's a tough role but one some journalists say prepared them well for later positions.

Anchors have a very important role. They're the faces of a TV news network, and they have a lot of responsibility. Here's some of what they do:

- **Introducing reporters' stories:** Anchors serve as the host of news shows, bringing reporters' stories in and also transitioning out of them and onto the next thing to air.
- **Reading newscast stories:** Anchors read stories such as readers, voiceovers, and VOSOTs themselves.
- **Interviewing guests:** If there is a live interview with a guest, it's usually done by an anchor.

TIP

Similar to anchors, hosts guide viewers through shows. In video stories on digital publications and in documentaries, the journalists who are on-screen are often called hosts. But all these terms may be used differently, depending on the organization, outside of TV news.

People who are behind the camera

In every video medium, producers are key to success. Here are some things a producer does:

- **Booking hosts and writing questions:** Especially for talk shows or other non-newscast formats, a producer books guests for interviews and often writes the questions that hosts or anchors ask them. This is what is meant by "producing a segment."
- **Writing and editing scripts:** Many of the scripts that anchors and hosts read are written by producers. Producers of many levels often end up doing a ton of script writing and editing.
- **Managing people:** High-level producers often are managers in TV newsrooms and video departments. Not only are they helping to set the overall editorial direction, but they also help manage staff.

TIP

There are many levels and types of producers in a newsroom so this overarching title can apply to many, many different people. For example, instead of someone being called an *executive editor* as they would in a print newsroom, they may have a title like an executive producer.

You can, of course, also find many videographers, camera operators, technicians, and other people working cameras, editing tape, and getting stories on-air. These roles are essential, and their work often goes unseen.

TIP

If you're great at technical work, there are many places that offer technical certificates and other similar trainings to do this kind of behind-the-scenes work at TV newsrooms. These programs are labeled as TV production or digital media production programs.

People who run the website

Because the website is still key to even TV and video journalism, people must run the website. And, especially in a busy TV newsroom, there have to be people whose sole responsibility it is to keep the website updated. Oftentimes, those in this role have titles such as digital content producer or web writer.

Similarly, these tasks generally entail:

- **Writing and publishing stories:** In some places, not only do the people in these roles publish stories on the website, but they're often responsible for writing the website stories themselves. This is often based on video stories, but it can also be original stories that they report themselves, just for the website.
- **Archiving and publishing video:** After stories air on TV, they're usually posted online. This is sometimes done by a digital content producer if it's not done by the reporter or producer on the story or segment.
- **Posting and engaging on social media:** Social media is key, and getting those videos and video clips onto multiple social media sites, along with the proper captions and in the right format, is a ton of work. Additionally, they may do other things on social media, such as resharing posts from reporters who are out in the field.

IN THIS CHAPTER

» Understanding how audio innovation structures storytelling as journalists

» Learning about working in audio newsrooms

Chapter 16 Radio and Podcasting

Radio captures the age-old art form of oral storytelling — people using their voices to tell stories in a way that captivates an audience and pulls them in. As a medium, audio is perfect for journalism because it's used to:

- Share information easily.
- Grab the attention of listeners.
- Create dynamic stories.

In audio, the goal is to create what is called a *driveway moment* — when someone is in their car, listening to a story that gets so good that they stay in the car to keep listening even though they've arrived home. This is the type of work that many people think of when they think of their favorite audio journalism story.

In this chapter, I walk you through working in radio and podcasting, the different types of storytelling you can do as an audio journalist, and the various roles available to you.

Seeing Where You Can Work as an Audio Journalist

But working as an audio journalist can take many forms, especially today, as the emergence of podcasting and other on-demand listening has pushed more and more newsrooms to include podcasting as part of their main operations.

Today, audio journalists often work at:

- Public radio stations
- Podcasting companies that make long-form features
- Daily or weekly news podcasting companies
- The podcasting department of news organizations that primarily do other forms of journalism, such as newspapers, magazines, TV, or digital publications

Digital publications are often heavily print-based. But that doesn't mean they don't also work in other mediums. Video and podcasting are extremely popular departments to have.

Career-wise, the growth in these job roles has really helped journalists who want to go into audio have more options and more choices.

Understanding How Audio Differs from Other Forms of Journalism

Overall, there are some things that make audio journalism training different from for other mediums. Here are some of the areas that training homes in on:

- **Broadcast writing:** Audio requires writing that is much different from print writing. There is a greater focus on being conversational, writing shorter sentences, and using present tense.

- **Interviewing:** The quality of interview tape is essential. Listeners need to be able to hear the emotions in interviewees' voices, and the tape needs to be clear and easy to understand.
- **Natural sound:** Leaning into natural sound (referred to as *nat sound*) with your story is a key component in audio stories. Not only is it different from print, but it's also different from video because, with the absence of visuals, the listener relies solely on what they can hear. So using even more nat sound helps listeners envision the environment of the story.
- **Archival tape and footage:** Archival tape and footage can be extremely helpful in setting the scene for events that have already happened.

You don't often learn about how to look through archives in journalism school, but it's a skill you can learn from your friends who study history:

- Reach out to librarians at your local library for help.
- Look through the *finding aids* (documents that list what are included in archives and where) in any special collections that list what archives have and in what form.
- Ask about access and subscriptions to any databases that you can look through with your library card.

Listening on the Dial and Long-Form Audio Storytelling

Although the radio has been around since the 1890s, it wasn't until 1920 that the first radio broadcast ever took place when Pittsburgh, Pennsylvania's KDKA announced that Warren G. Harding defeated James M. Cox in the presidential election.

Since then, news radio has been a primary way for Americans to get news. It's a key form of disseminating news because it can transmit essential information to people in areas that are difficult to reach, such as rural areas; areas that don't have reliable internet connections; and *news deserts*, which lack sufficient local newspaper access. This has also made radio important in countries all over the world.

With over half of U.S. adults getting their news from radio, the growth in on-demand audio listening is not surprising. Traditional listening on the radio requires the audience to listen to radio programming at a certain time. But, now, they can listen whenever they want to:

- On a show's website, where they can stream it online
- On a podcasting app, such as Apple Podcasts or Spotify
- On a show or network's app, such as NPR One

This switch to using on-demand platforms to listen to the same and similar stories people can listen to on the radio isn't surprising. It allows people to take in the kind of journalism they love but on their own terms.

But there are some differences between radio and podcasting. Although the lengths and structures of stories on the radio generally stay the same as they must fit within important time frames, there is a lot more flexibility with podcasting and on-demand listening as long-form audio storytelling.

TIP

Many journalists who want to try audio work on it on their own. It's a way to figure out if they actually like it. Podcasting has a low barrier to entry and there are many organizations you can join that provide free and inexpensive training, mentoring, and resources. One such organization is the Association of Independents in Radio (`https://airmedia.org`). It's one of the most popular organizations for helping independent journalists get better at audio.

Identifying the Traits of Top Audio Journalists

Many top audio journalists have been trained in print writing basics at some point.

REMEMBER

Journalism programs typically require all students to learn how to write for print, even if they want to focus on another medium.

So, when it's time to shift to writing for the ear, that switch can be a tough one. It's helpful to think of it as an additional skill — one that's much different and used in a different way. Writing or audio requires you to:

- **Be conversational.** In order for people to understand what you're saying, you need to write how you speak. It should sound natural to the listener, and that requires you to write in a conversational way.
- **Make sentences shorter.** When you write, you generally make sentences much longer than the sentences you speak. If you don't make them shorter in audio scripts, it makes it difficult to read them and sound natural without stumbling. It also puts too many facts in a single sentence, and it makes it easy for your listeners to miss important information.

TIP

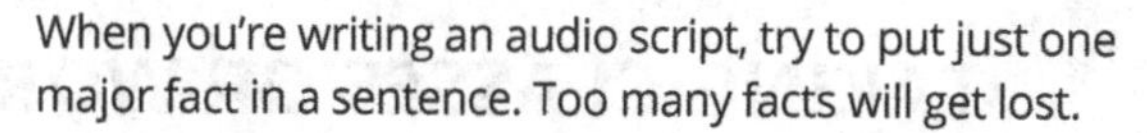

When you're writing an audio script, try to put just one major fact in a sentence. Too many facts will get lost.

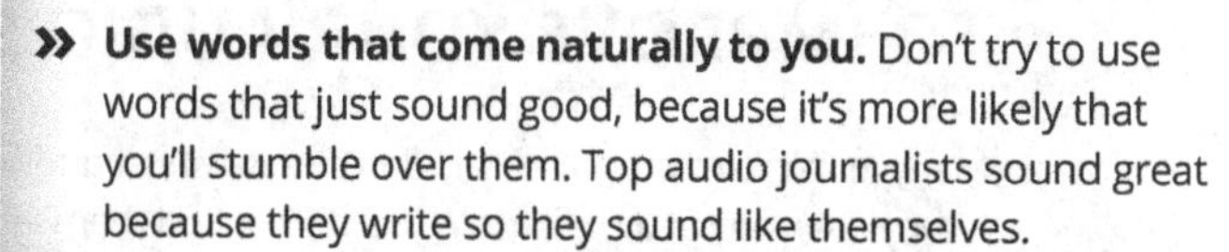

- **Use words that come naturally to you.** Don't try to use words that just sound good, because it's more likely that you'll stumble over them. Top audio journalists sound great because they write so they sound like themselves.

Writing is a big part of audio journalists' talent, but there are others areas that are important to think about, too. Here are some other skills that top audio journalists have:

- **Getting good tape:** In audio, you'll hear a lot of people talk about getting *good tape* (a high-quality recording that captures a good interview or a good scene). And that's because recording things in the moment and record them well is a skill. The success of your story relies on how much good tape you have, because it's the basis of what you can make.

» **Choosing strong quotes:** The benefit of audio is that you can hear interviewees, without distraction and with a focus on what they're saying. So, it's important to choose pieces of tape in which you can really hear how they feel about a topic.

REMEMBER

Choose quotes that show emotion, have specific language, and translate well for the medium.

» **Creating scenes:** The difference between audio and video is that audiences can't see where you take them. So, when you're able to create a scene for them — with your mix of words and the tape you have — you're able to help them envision exactly where you are in the story.

» **Knowing when to cut:** Especially with the invention of podcasting, you may not always have the same forced time limits on stories. But the best audio journalists know how to ask for and take feedback, work through the editing process, and know when to cut a story that may be too long.

TIP

It's always better for a story to be shorter and more compelling than for it to be longer and have boring moments, move slowly, or lose the audience.

TAKING CLASSES OR WORKSHOPS TO IMPROVE YOUR AUDIO SKILLS

Many journalism programs still don't have robust audio programs — if they have any at all. So, many journalists find themselves learning elsewhere. Here are some classes you can find that will improve your skills:

- **Story editing:** Editing audio stories is much different from editing print, and it's a skill you can learn through experience and teaching. Workshops around becoming an editor help create more editors for the industry. One example is Edit Mode by the Association of Independents in Radio (www.soundpath.co/

edit-mode), an "intensive paid training and mentorship program aimed at diversifying the audio industry's editor pool."

- **Editing tape:** Editing tape is different from story editing. Story editing focuses on shaping and guiding the editorial direction of the story, but these audio editing focus specifically on the production aspect — how stories sound. An example of a class you may take is Audio Editing by LinkedIn Learning (`www.linkedin.com/learning/topics/audio-editing`).
- **Pitching your podcast:** Many more people — journalists included — have created their own podcasts independently and then pitched them to media organizations after. Because of the popularity of this route, several workshops talk about pitching your project to podcast executives. One example is How to Make a Pitch Deck and Budget for Your Podcast by Radio Boot Camp (`https://radiobootcamp.org/classes/how-to-make-a-pitch-deck-and-budget-for-your-podcast`).

Structuring a Story for Audio

Structuring audio stories can differ greatly from structuring them for print. There is no inverted pyramid here (turn to Chapter 14 for more on the inverted pyramid).

TIP

Instead of thinking through the inverted pyramid for audio stories, think about how to create a more interesting narrative story:

» **The rule of threes:** This rule works even for very short stories in audio and is a great one for beginners. Balance out your structure by having three separate sections — like three acts of a play. You can create this feeling of three in many ways:

- A distinct beginning, middle, and end
- Three places
- Three time periods
- Three points of view

For example, a story that asks voters about their ideas on election day is more interesting when you go to three different polling locations.

- **A compelling lead:** Audio journalists are always thinking about how to keep people listening. The best way to do that is to have a compelling lead, and for an audio story, that includes more than just a first line. Think of the lead as the entire starting section of your story.

  For example, a compelling lead about a new program that helps people in debt keep their homes could be the audience meeting and hearing the story of a family that was in that predicament.

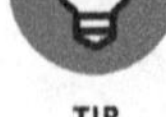

  Whenever possible in audio, show an example. Using stories and examples in lead sections does this.

- **Signposts:** Signposts are a way that audio journalists help listeners understand where the story is going. Think of it like actual signs that guide the audience along the way.

  For example, in a story that talks about a new student loan forgiveness plan, a signpost might be: "But first, we have to talk about why Americans have so much student loan debt." Giving this background may feel like going off topic so the signpost lets listeners know where the story is going and why.

  Longer stories will have way more signposts than shorter stories because more guidance is needed. You may not have any signposts in a short story that's less than a minute, whereas a story that's 20 minutes long will be filled with them.

In the following sections, I guide you through the various story formats.

News stories on the radio

The news stories that we often hear on the radio can come in many different forms. This is because just like when we're reading print stories or when we're watching TV news, stories serve different purposes — even stories that are all classified as news.

On any given hour, you may hear radio news stories that:

- Share breaking news.
- Give helpful daily information.
- Add context to more complicated news updates.
- Provide a platform for full interviews.
- Discuss entertainment.

When it comes to the form these stories take, it varies. Journalists decide which stories take which form depending on the:

- **Time in the story:** How much time is needed to accurately discuss the story is an important consideration. A complicated story can't necessarily be done well in a story form that is less than a minute.
- **Time the reporter has:** How much available time the journalist reporting the story has to do the story is always a factor. Some stories can be done quickly in an hour, whereas others require at least a day to do well.
- **Time in the schedule:** How much time is available in the schedule also matters. If there are many long features scheduled to air, for example, there may not be space to add any additional features without bumping one from the schedule.

Radio schedules are always changing. They could be moving until the very last minute because newsrooms work diligently to make sure that no essential stories are left out.

Even with a lot of variety, there are some very common types of news stories you may hear on the radio. As a listener, you may not have noticed these formats, but as a journalist, it's helpful to think about how they differ and their purpose.

Different newsrooms have slightly different times, and possibly, different names for these types of stories, but they're still extremely similar in description and fall around the same length.

Here are some of the common news stories on the radio:

- **Readers:** A reader is a short story that a host reads. There is no *actuality* (tape from an interview or another person). It is only the host. The length is short (less than a minute in most newsrooms). The structure is simple because there is usually just room for a couple of sentences. The purpose is to give listeners a quick news update, not outline anything too detailed.

TIP

A reader in radio news is pretty much the same thing as a reader in TV news.

- **Cut and copies:** A cut and copy may be referred to by other names such as a *wraparound* in different newsrooms. Either way, it's a story in which the host reads something, plays a short piece of tape, and then reads something else. A cut and copy is similar to a reader except it *does* have an actuality. The length is short (less than a minute in most newsrooms). The structure is simple because there is only time for a couple of sentences before the tape and a couple sentences after it. The purpose is to give listeners a quick news update, not outline anything too detailed.
- **Spots:** A spot is done by a reporter in a newsroom and is an edited story that includes the reporter's narration and actualities from interviews. It's all mixed together and played, not read live, like readers and cut and copies. The length is short (less than a minute in most newsrooms). The structure is simple because although there should be a beginning, middle, and end, there is not much time for very long pieces of tape or too many sentences of narration. The purpose is to give listeners a news update, but because it's preproduced, there is a lot of variety in the types of stories spots can cover — anything from news updates to event previews.
- **Features:** Features are the audio stories people think of when they think of the power of audio as a form of narrative. It's the story form that's known for creating those driveway moments. The length is much longer than other forms of news stories — usually somewhere between 4 and 12 minutes, depending on the newsroom. The structure can be creative but there must be an identifiable beginning,

middle, and end. The purpose can also be widespread — an audio feature is similar to a print feature in that way.

Most newsrooms set certain times that features need to be in order to fit within their news schedules. At the radio station I worked at, for example, features had to be either 4, 6, 8, or 12 minutes to easily fit into certain time slots.

- **Superspots:** A superspot is a mix between a spot and a feature. It's a story that may not have enough meat for a full feature but has more info than what can be in a spot. The length is between a spot and a feature, somewhere around one and a half and two minutes. The structure is similar to a feature, with a strong beginning, middle, and end. The purpose can also be more widespread.

Sometimes, a newsroom may air two superspots back-to-back so they appear to be together in what may be called a *pinwheel*. This tactic is especially helpful if there are two superspots that are on a similar topic or subject area. Again, this may be called something different in different newsrooms.

Podcasts and long features

Although the traditional radio feature may not be much longer than 12 minutes, podcasting has changed the limitations of the radio schedule. People can listen to audio storytelling whenever they'd like to, for as long as they'd like.

This change has meant that audio journalists have been able to be more creative than ever before. It's common for journalists to try one or more podcast projects — either as part of their work in their newsrooms or as side projects.

Here are just some of the types of podcasts audio journalists may work on:

- **Narratives:** It's easy to think of narrative podcasts as longer features. They're well-reported and the kind of award-winning podcasts that can make someone's career. Narratives are scripted and structured like a feature. They're sometimes episodic so episodes don't get too long and lose listeners' attention.

* **Interviews:** Interview-based podcasts are seen as *light touch* (an audio term to describe how much something is edited) because they aren't as scripted as narrative podcasts. But, when done well, they still take a lot of work. They're mostly unscripted, but the intro, outro, transitions, and questions are on a script. They're structured to complement the flow of a conversation, similar to a talk show. Interviews can be of any length.

  Although interview podcasts may seem to be easy to do, the best ones are anything but. The great podcasters in this area prep well for these interviews, do a ton of research, and edit the podcasts flawlessly so they feel as if the conversation were perfect. They are, indeed, work and they're absolutely edited for flow.

* **Chatcasts:** A chatcast is a type of podcast in which a host or multiple cohosts talk back and forth. Journalists don't often use this format for a full podcast because there is no real structure, but it could be a portion of a longer podcast. For example, there may be an unscripted five-minute talk at the beginning or end of something as a segment within a longer episode. Chatcasts are unscripted and unstructured, and they can be of any length.
* **Panels:** Think of a panel in the same way you would a panel event. A host or two cohosts serves as moderator(s) for a panel of people. They're mostly unscripted, but the intro, outro, transitions, and questions are on a script. They're structured to complement the flow of a conversation, similar to a live panel conversation. Panels can be of any length.
* **Game shows:** Radio shows have expanded into the game show format common on TV — with the most popular ones airing for an hour on some radio stations and all others living in the podcast world. Game shows are mostly unscripted, but the intro, outro, transitions, and questions are on a script. They're structured to fit within specific segments — for example, three segments of equal length. They must be edited down to an hour.

  One of the most popular game shows is NPR's *Wait Wait. . .Don't Tell Me!,* which films live in Chicago but also goes on the road. Attending a taping shows just how much goes into a show that sounds seamless when you listen to it. You can hear and see the hosts retake questions that need to be edited back in for quality, and you can see just how many producers are needed for everything to run. It's a reminder that shows need to be edited to be great.

- **Scripted fiction:** Even journalists can get innovative and create scripted fiction podcasts, often based on real reporting, real issues, or the creative expression of real imaginative solutions. As the name implies, scripted fiction is scripted. It's also structured and episodic, like an audiobook broken down into parts.
- **Call-ins:** Just as with a live talk show, some people have taken on this idea and created live call-in podcasts. These podcasts are mostly unscripted, but the intro, outro, transitions, and questions are on a script. They're structured to fit within specific segments, based on topics. Call-ins are likely limited to an hour or a certain time frame.

TIP

These formats are helpful when thinking through options for formatting a podcast project, but many of these categories overlap. You can also use multiple categories for different parts of a podcast episode or use different formats for different episodes, based on what you'd like to convey.

Looking at the Roles and Responsibilities of Audio Journalists

Newsrooms that prioritize audio stories have people who work together to create these products. Their jobs often fall within the following three categories:

- People who are on air
- People who are behind the scenes
- People who run the website

Although there are differences, there are many similarities between a radio newsroom and a TV newsroom. It's helpful to know this because, often, the names and titles of some roles can look quite different but have the same purpose.

People who are on air

Multiple people are often on air in an audio newsroom, but most fall within one of two categories: reporters and hosts.

Other people may also be on air sometimes, too. But in this section I'm talking mostly about people whose main job is to create content that is aired.

Reporters are the voices you hear quite often. When you think about the traditional newsroom structure, they're who you would see in almost any kind of media organization. They may cover different subject areas or different communities, based on how a place is set up. But they may have some slightly different expectations in a place like a public radio newsroom.

Here's what the role of reporter may look like in such a newsroom:

- **Finding stories:** Reporters' job is to be connected with the subject areas or communities they cover. And that entails going out to places and events to find stories.
- **Always recording:** Audio journalists always have their audio kit with their recorders in hand. They're ready to capture tape and sound at any moment, even if they aren't sure if they may need to use it yet. For example, if you walk into a room, capture its natural sound. You may need it for the story.

  Nat sound is integral to helping create a scene for listeners, so it's always top of mind for reporters.

- **Writing both audio scripts and digital/print stories:** One major difference between being an audio reporter and being a print reporter is the responsibility to write two versions of stories instead of just one. Because audio stories are written differently from print stories, writing a story for the website requires writing a virtually new story.

REMEMBER

Most newsrooms have a digital or online presence. This is the same for places such as radio stations. So, having a digital or print-style version of audio stories is often a priority.

- **Producing many of their own stories:** Depending on the newsroom, many audio journalists produce many of their own stories. That means that after writing the script, they record themselves reading it, cut the tape of this narration, and mix it into their interview tape along with any other tape such as nat sound.

  For longer pieces, newsrooms will likely have reporters work with producers to do this. But for stories that are a few minutes or shorter, it's more likely the reporter will do all of this by themselves.

Another person who is on air in a radio newsroom is the host. This is a voice that is extremely important and one that listeners hear quite often throughout the day. Here is some of the work the host does:

- **Reading newscasts:** Hosts read a lot of the news, the time, the weather, and many of the things people are tuning in to hear. They're an essential and trusted voice for listeners. They also do live and prepared two-way interviews when news breaks.

REMEMBER

  Hosts read short stories such as readers and cut and copies.

- **Ushering in reporters' stories:** Hosts introduce all the stories reporters have produced. They also transition out of those stories and into the next thing scheduled to be aired.

TIP

  Think of a radio host in the same way you do a TV anchor. Along with producers, hosts are responsible for keeping the show running because they introduce stories and end stories, flowing from one to another.

» **Hosting shows:** A specific type of host is a show host. Instead of hosting and introducing news like an anchor, they host a particular show. Prepping for that show, interviewing guests, and working on it specifically is a very involved job, so it takes up all their time.

TIP

A good and popular TV comparison to this is thinking of your favorite morning show. Those shows have interviewees but aren't really interrupted by news, and they don't really have prepared and reported stories.

Show hosts are the radio equivalent of the hosts of those TV shows. Both types of hosts are focused on interviews and talking to people. Radio hosts may try to do creative segments, such as reporting live from different places, but the shows are supposed to be interactive and often take call-ins from listeners. So, these types of audio shows are segmented in order to have a more conversational approach to news.

People who are behind the scenes

Many people work behind the scenes in audio newsrooms. You may not hear their voices on air, but their work is key to having smooth operations. Here are just some of the roles of people behind the scenes:

» **Engineers:** Engineers ensure that content gets on the radio. They know how the airwaves work and the proper format for everything. There is always an engineer on duty. Without them, there is no radio.

» **Producers:** Producers play many roles in an audio newsroom. Here are some of the responsibilities they may have:

- Producing long features
- Producing shows
- Scheduling when stories run
- Working closely with hosts

TIP

Similar to show hosts, show producers likely spend all their time working on their show — prepping for interviews, searching for and booking guests for interviews, and meeting guests as they come and go.

- **Editors:** Editors shape reporters' stories and make sure that everything is edited before it goes on air. They're essential in making editorial decisions, especially when they're needed on the fly because there's breaking news or something needs to change last minute.

REMEMBER

Editors edit the overall story while producers edit the actual audio.

People who run the website

Just as with other journalism organizations, audio newsrooms need people who run their websites because websites are essential to:

- Archiving audio stories
- Presenting digital versions of stories
- Engaging with audiences

In some newsrooms, these tasks fall to reporters and editors. In other places, they're separate responsibilities for a digital team, filled with digital producers and editors.

Website responsibilities usually entail:

- **Publishing new stories:** Publishing stories quickly and efficiently is also something that audio newsrooms prioritize. Similar to print-first and video-first newsrooms, this task often includes doing an extra read of the text, choosing photos if there aren't any, and possibly writing or editing captions.

TIP

For efficiency, some places have separate digital writers who write stories for the website instead of having audio reporters write both their audio story and their digital story.

» **Monitoring the home page:** Ensuring that stories are up-to-date and that the home page is fresh as news changes throughout the day is an important task. How often this is done may vary by media organization but some places have tools to help them determine what stories are being read. If not, they may have rules about swapping out stories every couple of hours, for example.

» **Posting and engaging on social media:** As newsrooms have learned more about engaging their audiences, they've realized that they can monitor how many people click story links to come to the website from social media. They also can learn more about how audiences are reacting to stories in real time. So, although it's not technically a part of a newsroom's website, posting on social media generally falls to this group of people.

IN THIS CHAPTER

» Understanding the role of social media in journalism

» Exploring the career opportunities of journalists who focus on social platforms

Chapter 17
Social Media

Social media is now an essential part of journalism. Not only is it key in how journalists share stories from other platforms, but it's also how they connect with audiences, listen to the public's needs, and create true engagement.

In this chapter, I walk you through the fundamental social media skills you need to have as a journalist, as well as how being a standout online can help you grow in your career.

Looking at How Newsrooms Use Social Media

Social media has changed the landscape of journalism. There isn't a newsroom around that doesn't implement some type of social strategy. Whether it's official or unofficial in a media organization, social media can't be avoided.

In fact, it's something that newsrooms now realize they must embrace. But for years, many news leaders saw social media as something that was ancillary to their operations, something that was extra. This thinking left many organizations trailing behind their peers in this area because they didn't fully embrace social media until much later.

Now, however, across the board, social media is seen as an integral way for newsrooms to:

- **Share work with audiences.** One of the most common reasons newsrooms decide to start posting on social media sites is to share the stories they produce. This has become especially important as stories live online and distribution means change.

  For example, when people pick up a physical newspaper, they read it from front to back or they flip through the pages to find certain sections. If people watch TV news or listen to radio news, they're listening to it in order of what's aired. But when stories are primarily online, it's not guaranteed that audiences will scroll through a site's home page, so social media is one way to reach them.

- **Listen to audiences.** Talking to audiences is just one part of good social media practice. True engagement means listening to what your audiences have to say. This process includes leaving space for their thoughts, their criticisms, and their questions.

  Some newsrooms may employ an actual engagement journalism strategy, which is a more formal way to ensure you're listening to and including the public. But listening to audiences on social media is an easy way to think about conversations. Simply taking the time to see what people are saying, taking those comments seriously, and responding to them can show people they're a valuable part of your community.

  Engagement journalism, also called *engaged journalism,* is a way to create better stories by involving community members in all steps of the reporting process. It involves having regular conversations with audiences, and those conversations often do end up happening on social media, but it's not a social media practice alone.

- **Target new audiences.** The people newsrooms interact with on social media could be completely out of their normal readership, viewership, or listenership. Without the normal boundaries of physical reach, it's common to have a social media audience that already slightly differs. But it can be an opportunity to bring these new audiences fully into the fold by creating stories that appeal to them and getting them to be a part of your core audience.

A good example of this could be age. If the primary readership of a newspaper skews older and it has been having a difficult time reaching younger readers, it could use social media to connect with them. Or, think about the geographic makeup of a city — a local radio station could use social media to connect with people who live in parts of a major metro area and work to convert them into listeners.

- **Find story ideas.** Knowing what's going on in the locations and subject areas journalists cover all comes down to what real people are experiencing. Social media is a way to see firsthand what those real people are discussing and get ideas from them.

  Social media users are often talking about what's happening in their lives, and on platforms like X (formerly known as Twitter) where the algorithms are created to be more of an open discussion forum, you can more easily see how people are experiencing certain issues. On platforms like Facebook, where people's individual accounts are mostly closed off to people who aren't their friends, there are still parts of those platforms such as groups and pages where people are more open and discuss issues with people who are outside of their normal friend circle.

TIP

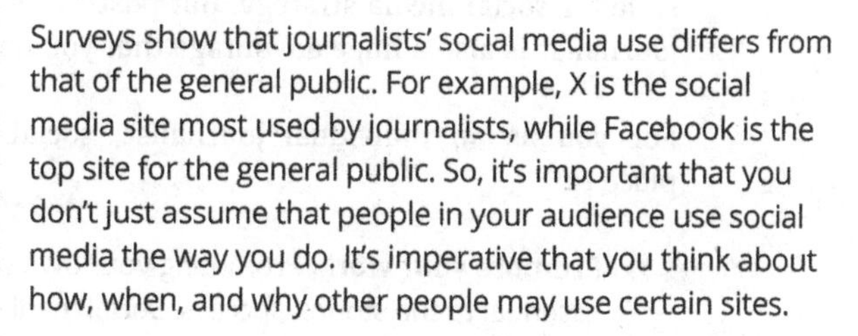

Surveys show that journalists' social media use differs from that of the general public. For example, X is the social media site most used by journalists, while Facebook is the top site for the general public. So, it's important that you don't just assume that people in your audience use social media the way you do. It's imperative that you think about how, when, and why other people may use certain sites.

- **Reach out to new sources.** Reaching out to people on their social media pages is sometimes a less intrusive way to connect with them. This is especially true when users have pages that are not private.

There may be some people for whom this is not the case, of course. But overall, people generally understand that being on a social media site means that people you don't know — including journalists — can reach out to you.

Before reaching out to a source on social media, take a peek at their behavior on multiple sites, if possible. If you notice that they're more active on a certain platform, try to connect there. This is especially important because, on many platforms, messages from people you don't know are filtered to a special folder that people may not monitor. They're more likely to see your messages on a site they use often.

Seeing How Journalists Use Social Media

Social media has changed how journalists work. Now, it's virtually unheard of for a journalist not to think about social media sites in at least some form or fashion in regard to their work.

Journalists post on social media in two separate ways:

- Using social media as a brand
- Using social media as an individual

Some people are employed by their newsrooms and are responsible for social media strategy. But posting as just an individual journalist is also a huge advantage that you have today.

For you as an individual journalist, social media can be a place to:

- **Promote your work.** Promoting your own stories is really essential to the stories' success. Social media gives you the opportunity to share your work directly with people who may be interested in engaging with it.

Although it may not be intentional, your newsroom may not promote your stories as much as it could. This may happen for a variety of reasons:

- **Limited time to post each story:** The social media team in your organization (or the individual person if you work for a small organization) may have a very limited amount of time to do these tasks. This makes it easy for posting on social to turn into a standard and quick activity that doesn't leave room for much creativity.
- **Other stories that take precedence:** Your newsroom may be publishing other stories that are higher in priority. So, the team that posts on social will be preoccupied with using any creative thinking on them.
- **Elements of the story that don't play well on social media:** Some stories are hard to translate to social. For example, if the story doesn't have strong images, it would be difficult to share it on X or Instagram and grab people's attention.
- **Lack of knowledge on the best ways to promote the story:** Not everyone knows how to communicate stories, what they're about, and what will appeal to audiences on social media. This can be especially true when people are trying to do it for stories they didn't report.

But even if your newsroom promotes your story to the max, there are likely people on social media who will reshare, read, view, watch, or listen to your work just because *you're* the one who shared it. In other words, they're a supporter of you and your work, not necessarily the news organization you work for.

REMEMBER

You're the biggest cheerleader of your own work. Share your work — and then share it again.

» **Promote yourself.** Social media is also a place for you to promote who you are as a journalist. As you apply for jobs and other opportunities, potential employers will check out your social media to get to know you as a journalist, as a staff member, and as a person in general.

Hiring managers may not admit it, but having a strong social media presence can sometimes improve your chances of getting hired for certain jobs because it can be beneficial for the newsroom. This is especially true for certain types of roles, such as those that are on-air and require you to be the face of a station.

WARNING

In the same way your social media presence can make you attractive to a job, it can also make you *less* attractive for one. Many journalists have lost out on jobs because of what they post on social media. If what you post is authentic to you, it could indicate that those jobs may not be a good fit.

- **Connect with other journalists.** Journalism is a tough and unique industry. But it's so much better when you feel like you're working as part of a community. Building up your own community by meeting people on social media who work around the country — or around the world — is beneficial.

  There are often trending topics and discussions that are only for journalists, and being part of those discussions can be beneficial. Social media can also help you connect and have friends who work at all types of different journalism organizations. It's a way to find community, yes, but also to learn and know more about the overall industry.

TIP

  Your social media pages shouldn't be filled with only your own stories. Be sure to share other people's stories, too. This will help you build relationships with other like-minded people — journalists and other supporters as well. (LinkedIn may be a slight exception to this rule, but you can interact with others' work by commenting on their posts, liking their posts, and if their stories align with the work you do, resharing their posts if it feels natural to do so.)

- **Learn more about your beat.** When you're immersing yourself in your reporting beat (see Chapter 19), a large part of it is just being a good listener and an observant viewer of what's going on. You go to meetings, pore over documents, and read a lot. But one of the biggest parts of the job is talking to people, and social media puts you in conversation with people from everywhere.
- **Build your reputation as a professional.** When people look you up, your social media sites are often the first ones to appear in search engine results. Whether you want to be seen as an expert on journalism, an expert on what you report on, or an expert on both, posting up-to-date info on these topics shows you're in the know.

TIP

Think about your friends who seem to know everything. You want to be *that* friend — and often, as a journalist, you are. You take in a great deal of information because you're always reading, listening to, and watching the news. Take a moment to post on social media whatever you find interesting. For example, some journalists are known for great analysis of sports and entertainment, while others are known for being the first to know when news breaks in politics. And this can be the case even if those areas aren't your reporting beat.

In addition to opening up the ability to have a strong personal brand, social media has actually created new careers for journalists. Many journalists who work independently, without the support of newsrooms, use social media sites to primarily post their work.

REMEMBER

Many people have chosen to abandon newsroom life to work as independent journalists. If you can't find a role in a traditional organization that's a good fit, social media is a way to not let a lack of job opportunities stop you from doing the work you want to do.

These independent social media journalists may:

- Create a YouTube channel as a main site.
- Lean on TikTok to post shorter videos.
- Go live on Instagram during protests.
- Create long threads on X to post updates.
- Tie in a Patreon, Substack, or other website to their plans in order for people to be able to subscribe to their work and financially support them.

TIP

One of the biggest hurdles of being an independent journalist is funding the work and making it financially feasible. In addition to websites that allow you to set paid subscription levels such as Patreon and Substack, more social media sites are starting to implement subscription models. For example, Instagram now has a subscription option where creators can post certain subscriber-only content.

Identifying What Top Journalists Do Well on Social Media

Although the standards and quality of posting on social media should be the same as publishing journalism on any medium, there are still some specific practices that require you to be really in tune with trends, people, and behavior. Social media moves quickly, so certain traits can bring success on these platforms.

Whether you primarily work in social media or incorporate it into your daily responsibilities, here are some tips on using social media effectively:

- **Have an audience-first mindset.** Thinking about the audience you're aiming to attract and engage with online is key to being able to work well on social and create content that resonates with people.
- **Recognize user behaviors.** One essential part of being a journalist on social media is being able to identify and understand how users actually use various platforms. Not all sites are viewed and used the same, so it's important to know just how people use them.
- **Keep up with changing trends.** How people use social media platforms today can change tomorrow. It's crucial that journalists recognize that social media platforms are continuously changing — don't rely on stale strategies.
- **Be an early adopter.** Journalists are often the first people to use new social media platforms. They aren't afraid to try them out, even if none of their friends have given them a go yet.

In addition to social media platforms themselves changing, how people use the platforms also changes. Think about the early days of Facebook — it was common for users to post statuses that were mundane updates like: "Arionne Nettles is thinking about writing." Today you'd never see anyone post a status in that way. People's behavior on Facebook has changed, and so have their expectations. Your job is to recognize all these changes as they happen.

- **Lean into authenticity.** Being authentic is key to success on social media. Audiences can quickly sniff out any fakeness so it's important that journalists — as individuals and as newsroom accounts — stay true to who they represent.
- **Be strategy-minded.** People who don't take social media seriously may think that you don't need a strategy for it. That's truly not the case. It's important view social media not only as a place for sharing but also as a separate medium that requires a formal strategy that answers the following questions:
  - What social media sites will provide the best benefit to our newsroom?
  - What are people's expectations on these sites?
  - Who are the different user groups we can target on these sites?
  - When and how should we post?
  - What resources do we need to be able to implement this strategy?
- **Reimagine content.** The best journalists on social media know that the way people take in information differs greatly by platform. And because your goal is to inform the public, you need to think creatively about new ways to share your reporting. Social media allows you to do this, but it often requires you to reimagine your work into new forms, such as:
  - Photo galleries and slideshows
  - Short explainer videos
  - Text threads
  - Blog posts that take readers behind the reporting
  - Images with quotes and statistics
  - Audio clips
- **Don't try to be perfect.** It may seem antithetical to most of what you do as a journalist, but social media requires a bit of risk. If you're posting in a new format, for example, it may mean that you put a lot of work into something, and it

takes a while to get it right. You may have to continue to modify certain aspects of your social media posts until you get the engagement you're hoping to get.

Some things to consider include:

- Language and voice
- Length
- Color and aesthetics
- Post time

REMEMBER

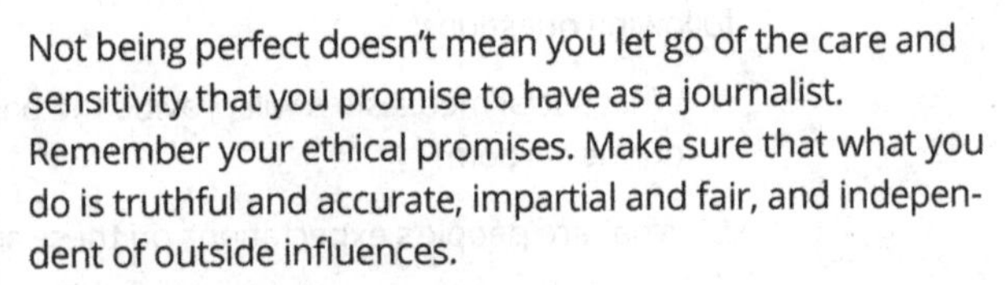

Not being perfect doesn't mean you let go of the care and sensitivity that you promise to have as a journalist. Remember your ethical promises. Make sure that what you do is truthful and accurate, impartial and fair, and independent of outside influences.

» **Don't take criticism personally.** Being on social media as a journalist is similar to reading the comment section of an online article: You'll see all the criticism, fair and otherwise, that people have about you and your work.

Handling negative comments on social media is something journalists should be prepared for. They're inevitable.

TIP

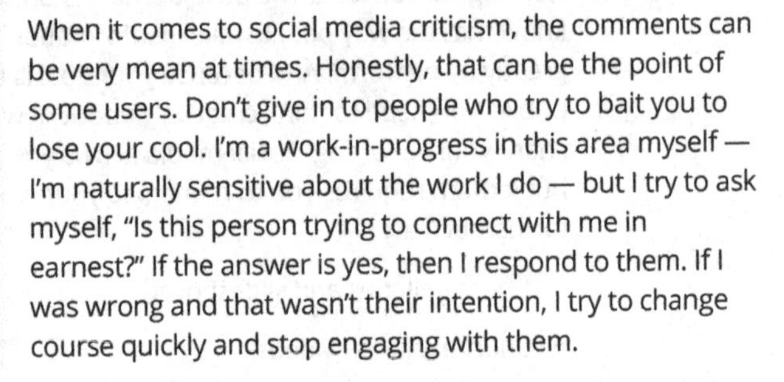

When it comes to social media criticism, the comments can be very mean at times. Honestly, that can be the point of some users. Don't give in to people who try to bait you to lose your cool. I'm a work-in-progress in this area myself — I'm naturally sensitive about the work I do — but I try to ask myself, "Is this person trying to connect with me in earnest?" If the answer is yes, then I respond to them. If I was wrong and that wasn't their intention, I try to change course quickly and stop engaging with them.

TIP

Before I was a journalist, I worked in digital marketing and ran social media strategies for companies in a multitude of different industries. I had no idea how much those skills would benefit me in journalism. But I found that having that experience and my ability to adapt to new social media platforms that weren't even around before I came into the industry helped me become a valued member of many teams in the newsroom. It also made me pretty fearless to try new things online to see if they worked.

CLASSES OR WORKSHOPS TO IMPROVE SOCIAL MEDIA SKILLS

Being not just competent but skilled on social media can give you a significant advantage in a newsroom — especially in one that may be struggling to create a strong strategy for itself. Here are the types of classes or workshops that can help you get ahead:

- **Social media analytics:** Analytics help you understand who you're actually talking to and what content you post that people may enjoy the most. Many people ignore actual analytics. Social media sites often host courses on how to best read their analytics; you can find courses on this subject from other third-party companies as well. Many digital marketers take these courses to monitor the social media activity of their brands. An example is the Social Media Data Analytics course by the University of Washington, offered through Coursera (`https://www.coursera.org/learn/social-media-data-analytics`).
- **Mobile video production:** When you're thinking about how to make video for social media, you're thinking about *mobile-first video* (video that will likely be viewed on phones instead of on computers). Shooting video for multiple social media sites is a skill. Mobile video production courses can give you tips and tricks to do it well. One such class is the Mobile Journalism Certificate course by Smart Film School (`https://www.smartfilmschool.com/courses/mobile-journalism`).
- **Breaking news on social media:** Breaking news requires a high level of thought and skill, and doing it on social media is something that even some seasoned journalists still get wrong at times. The rush to be the first to post can cause some journalists to forget the proper steps of verifying accurate information and fact-checking. But many journalism organizations have workshops and courses around how to do this better. An example of a course that covers verifying information online during breaking news is the Digital Investigation Techniques courses that are offered by global news agency AFP with the Google News Initiative (`https://digitalcourses.afp.com/`).
- **Audience engagement:** Audience engagement isn't solely done on social media. It should entail journalists going out into

(continued)

(continued)

communities and talking to people. But social media *is* often a key part of an overall audience engagement strategy because of how you can connect with so many people virtually. Because this field is relatively new, these workshops and courses are often held as part of journalism conferences and meetings, so look for them there.

Telling Stories Online

How journalists tell stories online is different from the way they do it in other mediums. It takes into account all of what we know about print, audio, video, and images and wraps all that into what we know about individual platforms and mediums.

In the following sections, I walk you through how to think through online storytelling. I also help you consider the differences in mediums and what kind of content is better for audiences on each.

Starting a strategy for social media stories

When it comes to how stories should be told online, think critically about how people take in information and be creative in your approach. It's not enough, for example, to simply share screenshots of a story when you can think through a better way of doing it.

TIP

Users on social media platforms want the content of stories and informational updates to:

- **Be concise and not too wordy:** Too many words are hard to read on a screen at once.
- **Use fonts that are easily readable:** Fancy fonts don't always translate well.

- **Be designed for easy reading:** The colors and spacing should ensure that users don't have to struggle to read captions and other words on images and videos.
- **Be easy to consume on mobile:** Most users are consuming the content via their phones.

The stories you share on social media will look different, yes. But retelling them well requires you to think about the essence of the story and how it may be different for different mediums. In addition to thinking about how what you share looks, think about how the content of your stories translates to social media sites.

Some questions you can ask yourself during this process could be:

- If I had to boil my story down to one sentence, what would it be?
- What are the main points of the story that would stick with the audience?
- Is there any information that I should leave out because it would be confusing if I can't fully explain it?
- Are there any real-life examples — with real-life people — that audiences can connect to?
- Are there any supporting statistics or facts that are key to the story as a whole?

Thinking through the differences in social media platforms

When you've determined the key points of your story, the next step is to figure out what form it should take on each platform you plan to post it on. Every social media platform is different — with different features that result in different behaviors from its users and different norms. That means that your audience has different expectations of what makes a good post on each of these platforms.

The creators of top social media platforms often try to one-up each other, copying and re-creating features that become popular on competitors' platforms. But even so, the platforms aren't carbon copies of each other.

An example of this is when Meta rolled out Threads, a companion app to Instagram that was meant to directly compete with X. But Threads, although it may appear to be similar, doesn't have the same user behavior as X. Similarly, Reels, which is Instagram's feature meant to compete with TikTok, is not the same as TikTok. Make sure you're aware of these differences.

TIP

When it comes to posting on multiple platforms, you can take valuable pointers from influencers. You may notice that popular influencers post very similar content on multiple sites, but they take the time to tweak the language or format to better fit the needs and expectations of users on those individual sites. These small changes may seem trivial, but they can make a huge difference.

As a starting point, when you're thinking about what form your stories can take, think about posting on social media based on the most popular types of stories in each format. Even with sites that have multiple sections you can post to, there is still some continuity in expectations. (For example, Instagram's Stories, Reels, and regular posts all can handle video, even though Reels is truly for video only and not still images.)

REMEMBER

When you're posting stories as a journalist, you can be telling stories on your own account or telling stories on your news organization's account. The process is similar — you should put just as much thought, effort, and care into posting on your own social media pages as you do on your newsroom's pages.

Considering whether the platform prioritizes visuals or text

Every social media platform falls in one of the following categories:

- **Those that are visual first:** Examples include Facebook, Instagram, and TikTok.

» **Those that are text first:** Examples include X and LinkedIn.

These categories work not only for current popular sites (like those I list here) but are likely to help you think through your strategy for new social media platforms that haven't arrived yet. This thought process of prioritizing whether text or visual content works best on a platform helps you get started regardless of who you're posting for.

In the following sections, I offer tips on telling stories on both types of platforms.

Visual-first platforms

On some platforms — such as Facebook, Instagram, and TikTok — visual content reigns supreme.

Here are some tips for posting on these sites:

» **Video is often king.** This is a very general statement, but overall, video does well on visual-first platforms, especially when the content is compelling. So, if you have some great video, prioritize editing it for these sites.

» **Don't forget captions.** Whenever you post a photo or video, you'll need captions. Not only does the caption make your content accessible, but many people say they watch social videos with the sound off. So, adding captions helps them watch the video when they aren't in a position to listen to any audio.

Most sites have a way to add automatic captions to videos, and you can usually edit these for accuracy. But to keep things simple, I usually add captions in the video editor I'm using to create the video. That way, I don't have to add captions on every single platform, and I don't run the risk of forgetting either.

» **Mix formats.** Try both video and photo posts. You're not limited to a single one, so use a mixture. You might find that some posts perform better than others or that your audience enjoys both kinds of posts in different ways.

- **Transform words into images or videos.** You can make quotes into images or even get creative and have moving text turn into a video in order to make messages more palatable for these platforms.
- **Let go of traditional editing practices in favor of social media trends.** The way you edit visual content for normal journalism stories doesn't have to be how you edit it for social media. The old rules don't apply. Instead, lean into any trends that may go against those traditional rules.

  For example, in traditional video editing, you never have *jump cuts* (a type of cut in which you break a shot sequence and the viewer can easily see that you made a cut because it jumps to the next part). In social media videos, this is actually a stylistic choice that you often see used.

TEXT-FIRST PLATFORMS

Some social media platforms, such as LinkedIn and X, thrive on text. Although they can handle photos and videos, they're known for being places where people have discussions.

Here are some specific tips for posting on these platforms:

- **Present information in a way people can absorb it.** It's tempting to simply copy and paste everything from a story on your newsroom's site, but don't. Think about how to best write or rewrite it to meet the needs of users of that social media platform.

  If you're really stuck and unsure of what to say for your post, pull from your lead and rewrite it. Your nut graph (see Chapter 14) is also a good place to look for the main point of your story so you can have a starting point to then write something into a tone and voice that matches social media.
- **Ask questions.** People love to use these social media platforms for discussion. So, if you ask your audience the right questions, you may be able to generate a lot of good interactions.
- **Switch up your language.** Never use the same exact language in multiple posts. Instead, think of different ways to express these points. Some sites also may not let you

post the exact same language multiple times, or they may show you lower in people's algorithms and you'll notice less traffic on subsequent posts.

TIP

It can be helpful to write all these potential posts in one document so you can see them next to each other. That way, you can edit them as a collective and then copy and paste them into the posts when you're ready to publish them.

» **Pick different parts of the story to highlight.** Especially if your story is making multiple points or if you have multiple interviewees who are strong examples of an issue, use each one as a separate post. Use their individual stories as a way to discuss the greater story.

TIP

Remix your behind-the-scenes content for your social posts. For example, the quotes you didn't use and the video that was cut out of the main story can make great social content.

SOCIAL MEDIA NORMS THAT ALL JOURNALISTS SHOULD UNDERSTAND

Even if you aren't a person who is technically on the social media or digital team in your newsroom, there are certain social media norms that all journalists are expected to understand.

- **You will always be a representative of your newsroom.** People in other industries may have the ability to not represent their jobs, but you do not. Wherever you are online, people will view you as a journalist who works for a media organization. And when they get upset with you, they'll contact your employer. This is very common.
- **What you tweet is taken as fact.** You're a journalist, so what you tweet — even when you're off the clock — is seen as true. For example, if you reshare something, people will assume that you're resharing from a source that you trust and that they can trust, too.

(continued)

(continued)

- **You can post during the reporting process, but it should be what you know.** If you share something while you're out reporting, it should be something that is confirmed to be true. You don't want to ever spread any misinformation.

  You can delete mistakes or factual errors on social media and correct the error by explaining what the mistake was in the same way that you would for a correction on a story. But if people have already screenshotted and reshared the mistake, it can spread quickly — even if you try to correct it. So, be careful to avoid such errors when you can.

- **Think about what your boundaries and limits are for your personal posts.** Post what feels authentic to you. There is no singular rule for what you should post as a journalist in regard to personal info. But you should know what your own boundaries are.

Most newsrooms have a social media policy that all employees must abide by. Sometimes, this policy can be a bit vague. If you're new to a media organization, it can be helpful to follow other journalists who work there and see how they post before you start. Also, keep in mind that a star journalist who is very popular and brings in a ton of accolades for a newsroom could have more leniency in what they post than the average employee. If you're unsure of what you may have posted on your accounts in the past, especially if you've had them since you were a teenager, it may be best to delete all your past posts or start new accounts altogether.

Posting Online for Your Newsroom

The responsibility of managing social media in a newsroom can go to a specific social media or digital team or it can be spread among many people across the newsroom. Nowadays, the job is typically concentrated and falls on a single team so there is some consistency in how the newsroom's social media strategy is executed.

On social media, members of this team:

- Plan, create, and publish posts.
- Respond to questions and concerns.
- Perform research for the newsroom.
- Follow partner newsrooms as well as competitors.
- Look at analytics.

In many newsrooms, there is a team of people that covers all social media platforms. But more recently, very large news organizations have started to segment their social media responsibilities even more. For example, the *Washington Post* has a team dedicated just to TikTok. Such teams also create original content for social media platforms and have the time and space to do so.

This organizational structure isn't currently widespread, because it requires a great amount of dedicated resources to pull off. But newsrooms that are able to have these kinds of roles have become known for their social media presence.

In many newsrooms, the people who post on social media may be the same people who run the website. That's because social media is often categorized as being part of a media organization's digital work.

Here are some other responsibilities that the digital team may have:

- **Publishing new stories:** Getting new stories up and onto the website must be done quickly and efficiently. This often includes doing an extra read of the text, choosing photos if there aren't any, and possibly writing or editing captions.

  Oftentimes, posting on social media is seen as being part of this process because a natural next step would be to use social media to alert followers that a new story is available.

  REMEMBER

  After posting a link to a story, you usually monitor how many people click on story links from that post and come to the website from it. It doesn't have to be a full-on look at the post's analytics — it's usually enough to keep an eye on the post to see how audiences may be engaging with it.

- **Publishing original content:** Oftentimes, the digital team also creates original content for the website, as well as for social media sites. They don't just publish and help with the work reported by others.
- **Remixing headlines and subheadings to use for newsletters:** Newsletters have become a huge part of how newsrooms reach audiences. It's necessary to rewrite part of stories, especially their headlines and any subheadings, to entice readers to click on stories.
- **Write social headlines and optimizing search engine optimization:** Some newsrooms have the capability of creating separate headlines that show up on social media, as well as separate headlines that appear in search engines such as Google. If there are any other search engine optimization (SEO) mechanisms available — link tracking, for example — they would also monitor those.
- **Monitoring the home page:** A newsroom's home page is important because the stories audiences first see when they go there determine how long they stay on the website. If they come from social media, for example, and then click around, it's this team's job to help organize the home page so there are fresh and interesting stories to grab their attention.

Some large news organizations have tools that can help them see what stories are being read the most to help them with this decision.

IN THIS CHAPTER

» Exploring jobs that utilize journalism skills outside of the newsroom

» Keeping the door to journalism open

Chapter 18 Working on the Margins

Working in newsrooms is a fantastic and important part of the democratic process. But many people who are trained to be journalists end up working in roles that aren't quite journalism. These roles are either on the margins of the industry or in separate industries altogether. But there's a common thread: Journalism training prepares you for many of these roles. After working as a journalist, you can:

- **Write well.** Not only are journalists overall great writers, but they're understand grammar, have a great grasp of language, and know how to choose words that really drive home the messaging they want.
- **Get to the meat of information.** Being a good writer also has to do with focusing on information and conveying information clearly without adding a bunch of fluff. Journalists work to ensure that writing is structured well and that the messaging is sharp.
- **Talk to people.** As a journalist, you learn how to talk to almost anyone — especially people you don't know. This skill isn't something that everyone practices in their field,

so it's a coveted experience and one that translates well to other industries.

- **Work on deadline.** Journalists know how to work on deadline and stick to tough timelines. They understand the importance of project management and can get their work in on time.

These skills are paramount in a variety of jobs. If you're looking for a job and you're open to exploring a job that's outside of a newsroom, you can look in areas such as marketing, internal or external communications, product management, technical writing, publishing, and editing. These are just a few of the areas that highly value journalists and journalistic skills.

Some jobs are very popular right now, and these are the jobs I cover in this chapter.

Writing Digital Marketing Content

Digital marketing consists of all the ways you can use the internet to connect with customers and other important stakeholders. Journalists are especially well situated to make and oversee smart and creative content.

Historically, journalists have always been attractive hires for content marketing roles for writing (for example, writing and editing college alumni magazines run by universities, or magazines owned by airlines). But now, many of these roles are primarily digital in nature. Oftentimes, digital marketing content is written, but it can also be in other forms, such as video.

Digital marketing includes things like:

- Writing blog posts
- Writing newsletters
- Writing social media posts
- Recapping events
- Ghostwriting executive posts

TIP

When you hear "ghostwriting," you may automatically think about books. But you can earn money writing everyday posts such as social media posts, blog posts, guest articles, and op-eds. A lot of what's "written" by CEOs and other executives is actually written by other people and just signed off on by them.

Digital marketing is different from journalism because:

- **You're working for the company you're writing about.** You are not unbiased. You aren't working independently from the company. You're creating content for the company, and you and your team are making things that are representative of the company's point of view.
- **Your intention is to make the company look good.** You avoid anything that's negative in this work. You highlight the good, and you don't talk about the bad.
- **You aren't looking for journalistic balance.** Unlike a journalism story, which often seeks to show multiple points of view, that isn't your goal in digital marketing. Your goal is to market a specific view of the company as part of its branding.

Even with these differences, though, so much of your journalism experience still applies. Specific skills from journalism include:

- **The ability to write in a certain voice:** Digital marketing content has a clear brand voice that should be noticeable regardless of what you're producing. This is an essential skill that people working in these jobs need because audiences require it.
- **Proficiency in using concise language:** Journalists can say a lot with few words. This is true for journalists trained in almost any medium, and that's an important skill to have in digital marketing.
- **Mastery of changing content for different mediums:** Just as in a newsroom, the best digital marketers know how to tell stories on multiple mediums. They know how to make the necessary changes and tweaks to make it work best for the form and the platform it will be on.

The way people take in information differs greatly by platform so your storytelling should change depending on where and how it is taking place. For example, a script for a video on Instagram won't have the exact same language as a blog post on a company's website — but they can be similar.

- **The ability to be a quick study:** Being a journalist puts you at an advantage because you're experienced in learning about information you may have never before encountered in a very short time period. You can accurately synthesize research and write about the billion-dollar budget, police reform, and midwifery in half the time anyone else can.

Creating Social Media Content

Social media content is made specifically for social media platforms such as Facebook, Instagram, LinkedIn, TikTok, and X (formerly known as Twitter). Although creating social media content can be part of an overall digital marketing strategy, many people are finding success in focusing specifically on social media content creation.

Here are just some of the ways creating social media content can be profitable:

- **Brand deals as an influencer:** Brands want to work with people who have strong followings on social media. But most important, they want to work with people who know how to leverage those followings and influence people to do things.
- **Consulting:** So many people recognize the importance of social media, but they have no idea how to use it themselves. Working as a consultant to people who need guidance is a way to share your expertise as a job.
- **Managing social media pages for others:** Many people pay others to manage their social media for them. That includes posting and engaging with their audiences. This task requires a lot of time, but because of that, digital marketers can rack up hours quickly working for clients.

- **Creating strategy and plans:** If you don't have the time (or energy) to manage other people's social media, you can still create actual strategies and plans for them to post themselves. Writing and creating posts and telling people when, where, and how they should post them can be a lucrative business.

Whether it's for companies or it's for yourself as an influencer, doing this work is nothing to sneeze at. Long gone are the days when the intern is the person at the company who is in charge of social media because they're young and know how things work. Social media is tricky, but because of the significant benefits of doing it well as a brand, it's financially beneficial.

There is also a link between how successful you are at posting on your own social media platforms and the opportunities that arise behind-the-scenes. Many popular influencers work with top brands as consultants, helping those companies boost their social media presence. They're often the secret weapon that consumers don't even know about. This type of consulting work is quite lucrative.

The journalistic skills that transfer well to social media content for brands include the following:

- **Conversational writing:** Writing as if you're talking to someone is always better for the audience than writing as if you're trying to impress someone with long sentences and flowery language.
- **Strong messaging:** Social media posts have just a few seconds to catch users' attention. It's important that messages are very strong and get across to them quickly and easily.
- **Experienced editing:** Regardless of what social media platforms you're primarily posting on, the job usually requires some editing of videos, photos, and more.

REMEMBER

On many platforms, video is king. So, prioritize getting your video editing skills in shape if you want to work in social media.

Working in Public Relations

Public relations (PR) is managing a company, organization, or individual's image and brand. It's an important part of a company or organization's operations, and it also helps individuals when they become so big that they need help managing how they appear in public.

PR involves:

- **Working with the media:** Media relations is an essential part of PR. This includes answering interview requests and other press inquiries, writing and sending out press releases, and requesting interviews on behalf of your organization or clients.
- **Serving as an organization or individual's spokesperson:** Sometimes, PR representatives step in and conduct interviews themselves, issue statements, and answer questions.

TIP

One of the most well-known roles, in this regard, is that of the White House press secretary. People in that position aren't working as journalists, but they often are former journalists and they use journalistic skills in their jobs.

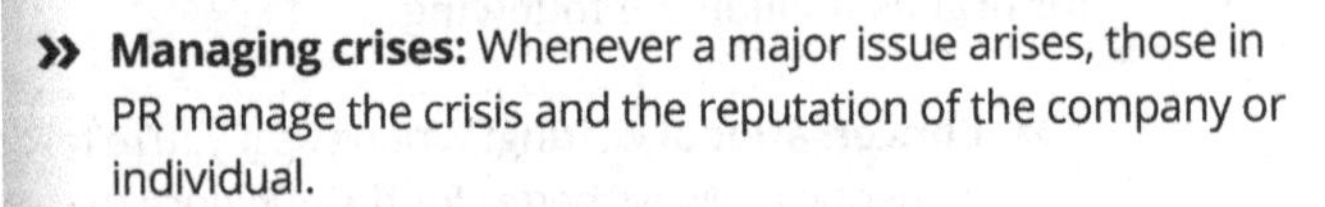

- **Managing crises:** Whenever a major issue arises, those in PR manage the crisis and the reputation of the company or individual.
- **Planning events:** Some people in PR also plan events. And if a company has a separate marketing or event planning department, which is often the case with larger organizations, the PR team will still manage the press that attends the event, as well as high-profile attendees on the guest list.

A lot of this job falls under planning and executing a PR strategy and accompanying campaigns. And it can be done in many ways, but mostly, publicists work in one of three categories:

- Working in-house for a company or organization
- Working for a PR agency
- Working independently for their own company

AVOIDING CONFLICTS OF INTEREST

Some journalists who go into PR want to keep the door open to go back to journalism at some point, so it's important to think about potential conflicts of interest and how to avoid them. Here are some tips:

- **Don't work for companies you may want to cover someday.** If you work for a company now, your editors may not trust that you'll be able to report on them fairly in the future. So, if possible, work for companies you wouldn't necessarily be covering if you return to journalism.
- **Avoid working in most political jobs altogether.** It's easy to go from journalism to politics. It's extremely tough to go the other direction. That's because most traditional newsrooms will think that you won't be able to appear fair if they hire you. For example, let's say you've worked in media relations for a political campaign. A news organization may assume that you wouldn't be able to fairly cover your former boss's opponent.

  This issue could be different in different types of journalism organizations. For example, having worked for a political campaign wouldn't be a dealbreaker for a job covering music at a music magazine, but it may still be a dealbreaker for a local newspaper that applies the same hiring practice across the board to everyone in its newsroom.
- **Keep journalistic ethics in mind.** Even if you're not working in journalism and many of the journalistic rules don't apply, think about the overall ethical promises that you made when you joined the profession. You can still be committed to truth, accuracy, and fairness.

Remember: You'll be working with journalists when you're in PR. So, you still want to keep a good relationship with them. Your reputation will follow you.

(continued)

(continued)

Other helpful tips to consider if you are in PR and want to keep journalism as an option include:

- Try to still keep fresh clips for your portfolio by freelancing.
- Stay up-to-date on journalism industry happenings.
- Keep your membership active in journalism advocacy organizations.
- Attend journalism organization gatherings and events.

5 The Part of Tens

IN THIS PART . . .

Get advice for covering a journalism beat so you can start your life as a reporter off on the right foot.

Get tips on how to write on any kind of platform or medium so you can be prepared for anything in this fast-changing industry.

IN THIS CHAPTER

» Immersing yourself in your beat

» Getting acquainted with key people

» Going out and being in the right rooms

Chapter 19
Ten Tips for Covering a Beat

Covering a *beat*, or subject, is exciting. It allows you to immerse yourself into reporting on a single area, which is something many journalists enjoy doing.

But beat reporting can be tough. You're often tossed into working on stories right alongside — or in competition with — journalists who may have been covering the area for years or decades. Yet, your stories are expected to be just as thoughtful, just as in-depth, just as well executed as theirs.

In this chapter, I offer ten tips on how best to absorb as much of your beat as possible.

Writing a Beat Report for Yourself

A *beat report* is a document you create for yourself that serves as a summary of information on a specific subject area. Writing a beat report is really helpful for getting to know your new beat. It pushes you to do research, yes, but it also creates a repository of information that you can quickly access as you need it.

Here are just some of the sections you should include in your report:

- Key institutions, leaders, and their contacts
- Summary of the issues
- Analysis of current media coverage
- Potential story ideas

Meeting Other Journalists Who Cover Your Beat

Covering a beat means that you'll likely see and work with the same people quite often. Just imagine working as a city hall reporter: Every time you go to a press conference, you'll be in a room with the same reporters covering city hall. Similarly, if you're a sports reporter covering an NBA team, you'll be working and traveling with the same reporters who are also covering that team. This all means that you'll be with the same colleagues quite often.

But as a newer journalist, or a reporter who's newer to a beat, you may need people to help show you the ropes. It's helpful to connect with other journalists — whether they're local or not — who are doing the same kind of work you're doing so you can learn from and with them.

TIP

Here are a few ways to meet some of those colleagues:

- **Join advocacy organizations and their task forces.** For example, the National Association of Black Journalists (`https://nabjonline.org`) has a sports task force for sports journalists.
- **Join professional organizations for those beats.** For example, join Investigative Reporters and Editors (`www.ire.org`), which gathers together investigative journalists.
- **Attend local journalism meetups, games nights, and sports leagues.** To find these events in your area, ask people in your newsroom if there are any teams or groups that they're a part of. Also, look for callouts on social media because these events are often shared within social circles.

Introducing Yourself to the Spokespeople of Small to Midsize Organizations

Meeting people in person and introducing yourself is the way to go when you're covering a beat. This is especially important when it comes to spokespeople and representatives you'll need to call and email later. Even if you're new to a beat, these spokespeople will be easier to contact than those at large organizations, and meeting them can leave a good impression that you're looking to build a respectful relationship with them.

REMEMBER

You aren't trying to be friends with the people you cover, but you should still work hard to build mutual respect. At the end of the day, you want to treat people with respect, and taking the time to meet people you'll likely be working with shows that you care about doing the job well and that you cover all bases. It's like introducing yourself when you start at a new job, except as a journalist, your professional field is quite large.

Getting on the Press Lists of Large Organizations

The spokespeople of large organizations may be a bit harder to meet in person than spokespeople of small or midsize organizations are. If so, it just takes a quick email to introduce yourself and get on the organization's press list. Generally, getting on the list and getting looped into what the organization is doing is half the battle.

TIP

If you're struggling to find the right person to reach out to at a large organization, look for past press releases. Not only do they help you see what the organization has been up to, but they always have specific people listed as contacts instead of the general department names and emails you sometimes find on an organization's website.

Going to Events Before You Need a Story

Reporting is an exchange — you're often asking people to talk to you and give you quotes so you also have to show that you're invested in what's going on. When you go to events, you get to meet people, see any issues or conflicts, and talk about what people would like to see in their news.

Going to events also helps with what to report on later. Physically being places helps you know what's going on and can help you come up with story ideas.

Getting Familiar with Past Stories

Knowing what other journalists have reported on for your beat is important — it's part of conducting a media review.

Here are some questions to ask yourself during your search:

- What has been recently published?
- Where have the stories been published?
- Are there any areas that feel oversaturated?
- What topics need consistent follow-up stories?
- What topics seem to be underreported?

Learning Special Acronyms, Terms, and Other Language

Your beat probably has language that's really specific to the types of stories you'll be reporting. So, it's essential that you get the hang of it. Don't be afraid to look things up and take notes as you commit these things to memory. Also, make note of how special terms are used. For example, if something is always abbreviated in a certain way or if it's more common to use an acronym than the fully spelled out term, note that for your story. This helps you write like the expert you're becoming.

TIP

If you need to learn a lot of specific language, make yourself a list with definitions and add it to your beat report.

Creating Google Alerts to Keep Up

Staying on top of what is being published about your beat can be a lot of work, but Google Alerts can help.

Here's how to create yours:

1. **Go to `www.google.com/alerts` and log in to your Google Account if you haven't already.**

2. **In the search box, type the words you want to receive an alert for.**

TIP

Use quotation marks around the words or phrases if you want an alert for that exact phrase. To narrow your search, use Boolean search operators such as *AND* and *OR* when creating your alert. For example, you might create an alert for *"San Francisco" AND mayor;* the quotation marks around *San Francisco* make it so you won't get alerts about San Diego, and including the AND means you won't get all results about San Francisco or all alerts about mayors — instead you'll only get results about the mayor of San Francisco.

3. **Click Show Options.**

Here, you can choose the frequency of your notifications (as it happens, at most once a day, or at most once a week), the sources (leave this on Automatic if you want everything), the language, the region (if you want to limit your alerts to a specific country), how many (only the best results or all results), and which email address you want the alert delivered to.

4. **Click Create Alert.**

Signing Up for Newsletters

Newsletters may feel like the new way for newsrooms to grab the attention of their audiences. But many journalists and journalism organizations are creating newsletters just for other journalists. For example, Study Hall (`https://studyhall.xyz`) is an organization that is run by journalists that shares opportunities such as jobs, calls for freelancers, and fellowship openings.

In addition to those newsletters, think creatively about the types of institutions that may have a newsletter that could be helpful for your reporting. For example, if you're a business reporter covering the economy, you may sign up for newsletters and email notifications from government agencies that release essential reports such as the Federal Reserve's research studies, as well as those from the Bureau of Labor Statistics, which produces the jobs report every month.

Picking Up the Phone

We live in an email-heavy society, and many new reporters avoid calling people. But beat reporting still requires journalists to not be afraid to pick up the phone. Journalists try to get the attention of people who don't know them, and quite often, email won't do the trick.

People are inundated by emails, and they may not respond to yours. Plus, good beat reporting requires you to have human connection with people. Because you're reporting on the same subject matter over and over, you need to view your sources as people with whom you're building long-term relationships, so you want to talk to them as much as you can.

IN THIS CHAPTER

» Writing with better structure

» Learning how to edit yourself first

» Tackling writer's block

» Leaning into resources that can help

Chapter 20
Ten Tips for Writing on Any Platform

In journalism, the most skilled writers know how to shift their writing for different platforms. They understand that there are essential differences in how people take in information when they're reading a print newspaper versus when they're watching the news on TV, for example.

But even if you know these variances, they all have important similarities. That's important to remember because, as the media landscape continues to change, there are some basics about writing that will likely stay the same. This chapter is a helpful reminder of those foundational lessons.

Thinking through Your Structure

Every single story should have a structure. That means that you should never just start writing without an idea of what that structure is — no matter how short or quick the story may be.

TIP

When thinking through your structure, here are some tips that work for all story types:

- Be clear on what your beginning, middle, and end will be.
- Start strong so you keep your audience's attention.
- Cut what feels like extra info and doesn't fit.

Writing an Outline Before You Write a Word

It may seem like an extra step, but outlining is really key to having — and keeping — a strong story structure as you write. Use the following three steps as a helpful guide to start:

1. **Outline your overall structure.**
2. **Add in your best quotes where you think they may go.**
3. **Fill in any other key info you already have.**

Using Words That You Would Use in Everyday Conversation

You may be inclined to try to use the biggest and best words you know. But most journalism stories are best when you do the very opposite.

Journalistic writing isn't the same as academic writing. Journalists mostly write for audiences of all educational levels. Journalistic storytelling requires you to make complicated things plain, and the best way to do that is to use the kinds of words you would use in everyday conversation.

That doesn't mean you can't use language to be specific and to be clearer in your explanations. It just means that every word should have a purpose and that you're more careful with your language than the average speaker.

Giving Yourself More Time Than You Think You'll Need

Great writing takes time. Great *writers* take that time. When you rush, you may want to skip the steps (such as outlining) that make your stories better. Rushing means you may pick the most convenient quotes, for example, and just try to finish. It's important that you build in extra time for yourself so you don't have to trade effectiveness for efficiency.

TIP

I set strict deadlines for myself. I give myself a certain amount of time to do each step so I don't look up, see how much time has passed, and have to start rushing at the last minute. This usually works even if I truly do have a limited amount of time. It helps me still make the best of it and not dillydally as much.

Getting More Information to Help with Writer's Block

Writer's block can feel debilitating. Sitting down to write and feeling as if the words just won't come is stressful. When that happens to you (and it happens to every writer from time to time), try to get more information:

- Do more reporting.
- Go over interview transcripts.
- Read through research studies.

These actions can be a huge help in getting you back on track.

If getting more information fails, just start writing. Start with whatever you have. It doesn't have to be the beginning of the story — you can always move things around and add to it later. But you need to get onto the page whatever you can.

Editing Yourself First

One of the biggest reasons writing may take longer than you expect is that many people don't factor in the time it takes to edit themselves. Every writer needs extra time for revision. After you finish your story, you need time to go back through what you've written and edit yourself. You should do this before anyone else reads your writing, and you should do it on multiple levels:

- Line editing for overall writing
- Reading your writing aloud
- Copyediting for style
- Fact-checking for accuracy

Even if you're working with editors, you shouldn't rely on them to ensure your story is good. It's *your* byline on that story, and you should do your own edits first.

Stepping Away and Coming Back Later

Writing is tough. It's a good idea to step away from it when you're struggling to complete a story and come back to it later. Instead of giving up, go for a walk, get a snack, and then come back to it. (The coming back is the important part!)

Taking a break from writing can also be extremely beneficial for editing yourself. When you're reading your own writing, it's easy to read what you *wanted* it to say and not what's on the page. This common practice makes it easy for people to miss their own errors and typos. So, stepping away and coming back can help you forget just a little what you wrote — just enough to help with editing.

When I'm writing really late at night, which I often do, my eyes glaze over a lot of my mistakes. So, whenever possible, I try to get up early the next morning to read over what I wrote with fresh eyes.

Using Style Guides

Style guides are essential in helping newsrooms have consistency in what they publish. But style guides can also do more — they can help inform your reporting processes, direct your language, and challenge your thinking.

The *Associated Press Stylebook* is the most popular guide for newsrooms, but it's just one resource. There are many other style guides, like those created by journalism advocacy organizations, that help reporters to be more inclusive in their reporting (see Chapter 14).

Reading Examples

There is absolutely nothing wrong with reading examples of other journalists' writing to guide yours. In fact, taking in a great amount of the kinds of stories you want to write is a way to study them. Essentially, you're analyzing good work.

To be most effective, look at the following things in these examples:

- The story's structure, paying special attention to how it starts and if it draws you in
- The writer's tone and voice for the story
- The emotion you feel when reading, watching, or listening

Trusting Your Gut

At the end of the day, you, as a journalist, know a lot about this story. You're the one who thought of the story angle, reported it, interviewed people about it, and wrote it. You're the person who's closest to this piece of work.

Don't lose sight of this in the writing or editing process. You are the conduit for the audience to know and understand what the story is, what the issues and conflicts are, and the perspectives of your interviewees. Trust yourself and your expertise as a journalist.

Index

D

L

M

N

O

P

Q

R

S

T

U

V

W

About the Author

Arionne Nettles is a professor, culture reporter, and audio aficionado who serves as the Garth C. Reeves eminent scholar chair and instructor for digital journalism at Florida A&M University. As a journalist, her stories often examine Chicago history, culture, gun violence, policing, and race and class disparities; they have appeared in outlets such as the *New York Times* Opinion, *Chicago Reader,* and WTTW. Before joining academia, Arionne held editorial roles at WBEZ, the Associated Press, and the *Chicago Defender,* one of the oldest Black newspapers in the United States. In addition to this book, she is the author of *We Are the Culture: Black Chicago's Influence on Everything* (published by Lawrence Hill Books/Chicago Review Press).

Dedication

This book is dedicated to all of my journalism professors and mentors, who built my foundation as a journalist; my own students and mentees, who encourage me every single day to be fearless in my decisions; and my current peers, who are putting in the work to leave the industry better than we found it. Journalism needs us to keep pushing.

Author's Acknowledgments

Without my acquisition editor, Alicia Sparrow, this book would have never been possible. I'm thankful for her foresight and for always believing in me. I'm so lucky to work with her for a second time on a book project. I'm extremely grateful to Elizabeth Kuball, my editor, whose care and dedication to making this book successful kept this train on its tracks. Her assistance can't be overstated. And, thank you to Ghazala Irshad, my favorite standards editor, and Adrienne Samuels Gibbs, my favorite story editor. They both served as my technical editors on this project and ensured that the content in this book was always in line. Many thanks to the entire editorial and production staff at Wiley.

Publisher's Acknowledgments

Associate Acquisitions Editor: Alicia Sparrow

Managing Editor: Murari Mukundan

Editor: Elizabeth Kuball

Technical Editors: Ghazala Irshad, Adrienne Samuels Gibbs

Production Editor: Saikarthick Kumarasamy

Cover Image: © SDI Productions/ Getty Images